Start a Cake Business and Make it Work

By Louise Wilson and Elly Russell

Published by
The Cake Makery, United Kingdom

Start a Cake Business and Make it Work
By Louise Wilson and Elly Russell

ISBN -13: 978-0-9934796-0-1
First edition published January 2016

Please note that all the information provided in this book "Start a Cake Business and Make it Work" is indicative only. No responsibility can be taken for errors or omissions or for any loss or expense incurred as a result of acting upon information contained within this book. When considering business commitments, it is always advised that you consult professional advisors. Figures and other financial information are correct at time of writing.

Start a Cake Business and Make it Work

CONTENTS

Start a Cake Business and Make it Work

Introduction

Interest in cakes and love of home baking is growing like never before. So too is the fascination with decorated cakes, cupcakes and cookies. The increase in the number of television shows dedicated to baking, cakes and cupcakes reflects this trend and is also fuelling the interest.

So, how do you embark on a career in cake? You might not be the kind of person, or have the time and/or money to start by attending a series of courses to gain qualifications. Some general knowledge and your baking and sugarcraft skills will get you started and there are there are many courses in sugarcraft and in business studies if you want add to your knowledge.

I learnt on the job and built my business while learning and earning money. You do need passion, and creative flair is always useful. You may have the option of working for someone else but many cake makers set up very successful home businesses allowing them to juggle other commitments whilst also reducing overheads.

As a cake decorator, you will be providing a service to individuals, couples and groups commemorating some of the most important events in their lives. It goes without saying that starting your own business, whatever it may be, will be very exciting, challenging and rewarding, but it will also be very hard work.

Hours of research, preparation and development will hopefully be followed by a real sense of achievement and, hopefully many years of successful trading.

Questions about starting a business and many related topics frequently crop up on our Facebook page and in our classes at The Cake Makery. We felt we needed to bring together a document which helped to address all these concerns in one easy to understand book.

These notes will teach you all you need to know to give you a head start. Hopefully our experience will save you much trial, error, and money as you go through the process of starting your own business.

Together we at the Cake Makery have over 30 years of experience running our own businesses in the worlds of internet marketing, photography, graphic design and of course cake decorating. You will gain from the benefit of our experience.

We know that it is a lot of information to absorb if you attended a course, so we believe that by providing you with this full and extensive book you will be able to learn at your own pace. You can dip in to particular sections in the book when you need to access that information. We also provide many useful documents, tables and contacts for your information. We hope this book will continue to be useful long after you have started your business.

Chapter 1

Where to start

Reasons for starting a cake decorating business from home:

- It is relatively fast to set up and you can start earning money straight away.
- Everyone loves a party, and there is always cake. There is definitely money to be made in cake making.
- Starting your business at home will keep down your start-up costs as you probably have much of what you need already.
- You will need to develop your skills but as you do, you will still find markets which will suit your goods. You don't have to achieve perfection before you can start selling your cakes and there are continually new and emerging markets.
- You may be able to generate much more profit as a cake decorator based at home, than in commercial premises.
- You'll enjoy the perks of being our own boss, deciding how much you want to work, what you want to do and when, how much you want to earn, when to take a break, a holiday and even retire.

Running your own business may not be for everyone.

Many people who run their own businesses say that it is about much more than just baking cakes. Keeping yourself organised is easier if you have a good head for figures and good time management. Some artistic flair will clearly help.

Hard work and good organisational skills are vital. You may need to work very long hours. You will have to be very organised to keep to your deadlines and yet maintain a cheerful disposition when dealing with clients.

Ultimately you do not want to lose sight of why you are doing this, i.e. your love of baking, cake decorating and all things cake!

Ask yourself these questions:-

Do I have:
Determination
Perseverance
Patience
Organisation
Understanding
Flexibility
Stamina
Commitment
Motivation
Self confidence
Enthusiasm
Willingness
Open mindedness
Ability to communicate
Ability to make decisions
Self discipline

Think about the pros and cons of working from home:-

Advantages:	**Disadvantages:**
Cost effective.	Interruptions and distractions.
Time saving.	Neighbour issues.
Flexible hours.	Isolation and lack of motivation.
Work around the family.	Impression of professionalism.
Home/family help.	Financial and personal security.

Ask yourself these additional questions:
- What will it cost you to set up?
- Do you have a budget or will you need to borrow for this?
- How many hours are you prepared to work each week?
- What is your target market and is there space for you?
- Do you have sufficient cake decorating skills to get you started?
- Can you do everything yourself or will you need employees?
- Do you need to make any alterations to your house to enable your business?
- Do you need planning permission?
- Who is your competition and how successful are they?
- How will you be different from your competitors?
- Do you have someone you can call upon for business advice?
- What are the risks if your business fails?
- How much money do you want or need to make?
- Do you have accountancy, marketing, communications and selling skills or will you need to source services?
- Do you understand computer technology sufficiently or will you need help?
- Will you need to develop or find assistance from others for any additional skills?
- Do you have a supportive family?
- If you are considering a home based business how will this impact on your family life?

Starting a new business may mean a temporary loss of any earnings and incur set-up costs. Consider how you are going to manage this in the early stages of your business. You may be able to obtain grants or bank loans. It is worth checking with the Job Centre, Business Link, the local authorities and banks for more information. See the section on Business Plans. If you're still keen, start planning!

A note on Action Plans

Setting out a clear action plan that you regularly review keeps you on track with ongoing projects and tasks. This can be immensely helpful in the initial stages of planning your business, as well as helping in the day-to-day running of your business. Giving yourself time scales focuses the mind on the day to day, while keeping an eye on the bigger picture.

The business plan

A business plan is a written document that describes and clarifies your business idea. It covers your short and long term objectives, strategies, sales, marketing and financial forecasts. You will need a business plan if you propose approaching banks or other bodies for financial or other support, loans, mortgages etc. It is a blueprint which should include phases of progress, forecasts and strategies. It can be used to review your progress at particular stages and compare what actually happened to what you projected. You can use it to modify forecasts and tweak your strategies as the business progresses. A clear plan will help you convince your bank, and other key providers, to support you.

Your business plan should include:
The "Management Summary" (also called an Executive Summary) outlines your business proposal and will be read by people unfamiliar with your business, so avoid language very specific to your trade. It should include the most important points:
- The product or service you offer and its advantages.
- How you see your position in the market.
- Your people (yourself, management, staff).
- Something about your track record to date.
- Your financial projections including your expectations for funding requirements, and returns.

A bank or other supporting institution may make their initial judgements based upon your Management Summary. The rest of your Business Plan will be studied by your potential supporters, to give more detail to aid their final decision. Appendices at the end of your plan should give more detailed information where necessary, to support the main body of your plan.

The main bulk of your plan should include details about:
- The background to your business idea, including what your product or service is, how it will be delivered to the customer and how it will stand out.
- How the business can be developed in the future to accommodate change.
- The key features of your industry.
- Your business's target market, including details of the market

where you plan to sell.

- Who your competitors are, and what the competing products are like?
- Your business objectives. Setting objectives will allow you to focus on the things that are most important in allowing you to drive your business forward (it is worth reviewing them regularly to ensure that you are on the right track.

The plan should also:
- Show that you have done the market research to justify what you say in your plan.
    - Pros and cons of your location.
    - Present knowledge of your competitors and how your product or service will compare.
    - Figure out exactly what you would have to charge to be able to make money.
    - Provide financial forecasts for the first two or three years
    - How do you justify your requirements for backing, and what exactly do you need finance for.
    - Explain how you will afford finance.
    - Indicate the facilities you will need to start and how much you will need.
    - Show how you will select your suppliers.
- Explain how you are planning your sales and marketing
    - How will you meet your customers' needs?
    - How will you position your product to the best advantage?
    - How do you plan to sell successfully to customers?
    - Will you be using advertising, PR, a website etc. to promote your business?
    - How will your profit be generated (different areas of your business might contribute different proportions of your income)?
- Explain your financial requirements - how much, what form, how it will be used and how you will afford it? Assess the risks - Look at your business plan and identify areas where things could go wrong, and look at the 'what-if ' scenarios, e.g. you get sick, your sales are 20 per cent lower than your original forecast, etc.
- Give a cash-flow forecast. As a cash business you should never have a cash-flow problem, but a forecast is important to identify any potential low cash points. It enables you to keep track of things, look at seasonal trends and consider where there may be cash flow issues.

Appendices
Detailed financial forecasts including monthly sales, monthly cash-flow and profit & loss, should usually be included in an appendix. You can add any other relevant information in these appendices.

Keep your business plan short and to the point. Most business plans are too long. Focus on what your potential readers need to know. Make it professional with a smart cover and a title. Include a contents list and re-read it yourself. Think about whether the person reading your plan will be given a good feel for your business. Ask your friends for feedback.

Your business plan will help you to clarify your business idea and spot potential problems. Use it to help yourself set out goals and gauge your progress. Example Business Plans can be found online which may offer you valuable insight to help you structure your own plan.

Business Ownership

There are essentially three recognised structures for starting a small business:
- a self employed sole trader.
- a partnership.
- a limited company.

Choosing the right one is important.

Self Employed, Partnership or Limited Company

Self Employed

Setting up as a sole trader, or freelancer, is by far the easiest and quickest way to start a business. It's fairly light on paperwork and does not require paying a registration fee, however it is paramount that you register as self-employed within three months of working or starting to trade. Failure to do so may result in a penalty of up to £100, plus interest on any taxes due.

Registration involves completing a CWF1 form to inform HM Revenue & Customs (HMRC) about your business. This will also register you for Self Assessment. Once this is done, HMRC will set up tax records for you and will send you a Unique Taxpayer Reference (UTR).

As a self-employed sole trader you will have to complete a Self Assessment tax return to HMRC every year. This involves filling in a tax return form, either online or paper, in which you inform HMRC of your income and capital gains, or in which you may claim tax allowances or relief. Your Self Assessment tax return can be completed online after the end of the financial year in April each year.

Partnership

The business partnership and individual partners must also register for Self Assessment with (HMRC) and follow certain rules on running and naming the business partnership. You'll need to choose a 'nominated partner' - the person responsible for managing the partnership's tax returns and keeping business records. The nominated partner must register the partnership and themselves for Self Assessment. The other partners register separately, they usually do this after the partnership is registered.

As a business partnership you are running a business as a self-employed individual but all the partners share responsibility for the business. You can share all the profits between the partners and each partner pays tax on their share of the profits.

Both the nominated partner and individual partners are responsible for sending in their own personal Self Assessment tax return every year. Each partner is responsible for paying income tax on their share of the partnership's profits and paying their National Insurance contributions. You are also jointly responsible as partners for all business expenses and business losses. The nominated partner must complete and send the partnership's tax return.

If you are Self Employed or in a Partnership you are required to meet certain Self Assessment payment deadlines. If you owe any money by the end of the tax year (4th April), you will be asked to pay that amount by 31st January the following year. The payment deadline is the same whether you file online or on a paper return.

You will need to pay one or both of the following unless you owe no tax:
- The balancing payment (the balance of tax you owe for the previous year).
- The first of two 'payments on account' (advance payments for the current tax year).

You should receive a Self Assessment statement that shows the calculation and the amount due. If you are asked to make payments on account, your deadline for making your second payment is 31st July.

Limited Company

Do you need to or want to be a limited company? Do you wish to remain as a small home grown business or do you imagine greater things? Consider this carefully depending upon how big your ideas are. Read all you can, about the sole trader versus the limited company to learn about the differences, the pros and cons and what will suit you best. There are two types of limited company – it is unlikely that you will be starting out as a Public Limited Company (PLC) traded on the stock market so we will concentrate on the Limited Company (Ltd), which are privately owned.

A limited, or limited liability company is very different from a sole trader. If you are a sole trader or partner, you can be held personally liable for any losses, debts etc. which can be met from your personal assets. Your liability is, as the name suggests, limited, with the limited company set-up.

Registering and running a limited company requires more legal administration than a sole trader business or partnership. However, a limited company is a separate legal entity to the company directors. Profits and/or losses belong to the company. The business can continue regardless of the death, resignation or bankruptcy of any of it's shareholders or people who run the business.

Limited companies pay corporation tax on their profits and company directors are taxed as employees under the Pay As You Earn (PAYE) system. People you employ to work for the company are paid in the same way. Your personal financial risk is restricted to the amount you invest in the company. But if the company fails and you have not carried out your duties as a company director, you could be liable for debts as well as being disqualified from acting as a director in another company.

Registering a limited company requires you to file the correct documents with Companies House before you start trading.

Note: You can also register a 'dormant' limited company with Companies House. This will allow you to retain a company name. This is useful if you are not ready for trading yet but wish to prevent anyone else from registering the same company name. As soon as you have significant accounting transactions in any accounting period, and these transactions are recorded in the business' accounting records you can no longer be a 'dormant' company. There is a small registration fee and an annual document processing fee and you would need to submit basic financial paperwork to Companies House annually but this is not the set-up for a fully functioning limited company.

Be aware that Companies House are very hot on paperwork and returns. They will be quick to apply fines and charges if paperwork is not submitted when required. They are also able to prosecute if the company's officers do not submit paperwork on time. Late submissions could also result in a company being struck off the register, on the assumption that it is no longer trading. The company would cease to exist and its assets would become Crown property. If you no longer require the company, you should contact Company's House to follow the correct procedure to remove the company from the register.

Note on accountants
Accountants can be a very useful aid when starting a new venture, particularly if you do not have much experience with finances. An accountant can be hired to help you manage just your personal self-assessment, but they can also be hired to manage all your business financial affairs if you need the service.

The Law

You must fulfil certain legal requirements before you can open for business. We have dealt primarily with the sole trader business model for the purpose of these notes though many of the requirements will be universal whatever type of business you run.

Informing the authorities

You do not need to register with Companies House when you start out as a sole trader, although limited companies do need be registered.

Anyone who becomes self-employed or who is part of a partnership, must register for income tax and National Insurance contributions with HM Revenue & Customs (HMRC) within three months of starting your business or you could be fined. The three months starts from the last day of your first month of trading.

Registration can be done either online, by phone or by post. It is usually far quicker and more convenient to sign-up online. While it is not possible to register in advance, it is important that you inform HMRC as soon as you start working.

Upon registration, you will need to provide the following information:
- Your name, address and telephone number.
- Email address.
- Date of birth.
- National Insurance number.
- The nature of your business.
- Start date of your self-employment.
- Business address - if different from your home address.
- Business telephone number.
- Your Unique Tax Reference (UTR) if you already have one.
- The business' UTR if you're joining an existing partnership.
- If relevant, the full name,address and date of birth of any other business partners

If you make all or part of your living by working for yourself, you are considered self-employed. As a self-employed individual, your tax and National Insurance contributions are not paid when you receive payment for your goods and services, therefore you are bound by law to declare your earnings annually to HMRC.

If you receive any payment for goods or services you have provided, or through a business you operate, this requires you to register with HMRC. It does not necessarily mean you will pay tax, that will be determined when the amount of your earnings are assessed.

Sole trader legal requirements

There are sole trader regulations and laws to be aware of, and certain trades may need a licence. As a home cake decorator, you will not require a trading licence, however you will need to register as a food business with the relevant local authority.

Take note of relevant regulations as dictated by acts of law:

- Trade Descriptions Act 1972: states it is a criminal offence to knowingly make false or misleading claims - verbal or written - about goods or services you offer. This includes factors such as ingredients, place of manufacture, customer testimonials as well as associating yourself with a brand without permission.
- Sale of Goods Act 1979: dictates that goods you sell must be of satisfactory quality, match your promises of performance and be as you describe them.
- Supply of Goods and Services Act 1982: commits you to undertake the services you offer with reasonable care, skill, time and cost.
- Data Protection Act 1984: directs you to protect the personal data you keep about individuals.
- Consumer Protection Act 1987: holds you liable if you supply a product which causes damage or injury, unless you can show that not enough was known about its dangers at the time of supply.

You should keep abreast of any legislation relating to environmental and health and safety requirements.

Business Name

The name of a business can be a valuable asset but some names might be detrimental to your business. Your business name **is** you and your business. It will be how people remember you, your products and your service.

It will appear in your advertising, your website, your leaflets, your business cards, stationery and on your products and services. You will answer the phone with your name. It will hopefully be passed on in recommendations to others.

Evidently, choosing a name is one of the most important decisions you will make when starting out. Think up a name which gives the right image. There are limitations in what is legally allowed, and you should be aware of these from the start.

You can choose almost any name you think of which conveys the right image for your business. Consider all the costs of stationery, advertising literature, boxes, vehicles etc. where your name will appear.

These considerations make it easy to see why it is important that you take great care choosing the right name. This will help you avoid the expense of having to change it. You want the name you choose to work well for you.

When deciding on a name consider:

- Will people be able to search for you easily on the Internet.
- Is the name easy to say, spell and remember.
- Does the name reflect what you do.
- If you want to protect your name by registering it with Companies House, you will have to check the name is available.
- Consider how the name might appear written or as a logo.

Restrictions

Certain words and expressions like international, federation and registered are restricted under the Business Names Act 1985 and the Company and Business Names Regulations 1995.

Companies House and the National Business Register have lists of these words and details of how to obtain approval to use them. Your business name can not be the same or too similar to that of another business, trademark or company. If it does conflict, you could face legal action from it's owner.

Check phone books, trade journals and magazines to ensure against clashes. You can run free name checks against all these via the National Business Register as well as the Intellectual Property Office and the Limited Companies Index at Companies House.

A solicitor can perform checks to be absolutely sure that you can use a name, or the National Business Register who will do the checks for you. You can also check for restricted words and names on their website at: www.start.biz/business_names/restricted

Registration

It is not a legal requirement to register a business name but you may wish to consider it. The National Business Register can take you through deciding, registering and protecting the trading name, ensure nobody copies it in the future or passes it off as their own.

You can register a Dormant Limited Company with Companies House simply to retain a company name. There is a small registration fee and an annual document processing fee. You would need to submit basic financial paperwork to Companies House annually.

Display of your business name

Your customers and suppliers have a legal right to know who is running your business and what the registered address is.

The Business Names Act 1985 requires every business to print this information on invoices, orders, receipts and letterheads, and to display it prominently at all business premises.

Sole trader
A sole trader using their own name, without any additions, has no special obligations under the Business Names Act (for example, John Smith trading as 'John Smith').

Other Names
If you are going to trade under a name different to your own personal name you must also display the name/s of the owners and an address where documents can be served. The business name and details need to be on all business stationery, letterheads, business cards etc. and at your premises.

Business Stationery

When designing your company stationery there is more to consider than just the design and the quality of paper. Your stationery needs to follow several legal requirements. Valuable cash can easily be wasted in overlooking these requirements. The requirements are simple, but vary depending on the type of business.

Sole trader business stationery guidelines

You can trade under your own name, or you can choose a different business name. If you choose a business name that is not your own name, you must include your own name and the business address on all letterheads and order forms.

Partnership business stationery guidelines

If you are a partnership business your letterheads, order forms, receipts and even invoices must include the names of all partners and the address of the main office. If there are many partners then it is also acceptable to state where a list of partners may be found.

Limited company business stationery guidelines

If you are trading as a limited company, the letterhead and order form stationery must include:

- Your full registered company name, company registration number and place of registration.
- The company's registered address and the address of its place of business, if different.

There is no need to include the names of the directors on the letterhead for a limited company, but if you choose to name directors all directors must be named.

Most letterheads also include telephone, fax, URL for the business' website and an email address.

Chapter 2

<u>Money Matters</u>

Money and finance, accounting etc. can seem quite daunting but they need not be overwhelming if they are carefully managed. Try to stay well organised, keep your paperwork in order and up to date. Make a note of, and deal with any tax or self-assessment items well in advance of the deadline so that you have adequate time to prepare for them.

If you have your product or service, a business plan, and a cash flow (however tiny), you will be in a position to look for funds for your business. You will need to be clear about exactly how much money you need and identify what you wish to use the loan for.

For small amounts of several hundred pounds, you could consider using a credit card or possibly borrowing from friends or family.

For larger amounts contact financial institutions e.g. banks. Many institutions will have a small business advisor specifically to help small businesses and start-ups.

Self Assessment

As a sole trader, you are self-employed and your profits are taxed along with any other income you receive, by the HM Revenue & Customs (HMRC). The process used is called Self Assessment.

The amount upon which you will have to pay tax is calculated by deducting business expenses and personal allowances from your income to find your profit. You will be taxed on your calculated income at the current income tax rate set by the Government. You will be required to pay your income tax twice a year. It is advisable to budget for this, putting money aside for the tax payments due in January and July each year.

As a self-employed person, many of your business expenses can be deducted from your taxable income, including overheads on your premises, travel, delivery costs and trade association subscriptions. Remember that you will have to pay Capital Gains Tax on any assets you sell or give away.

National Insurance

If you are self employed, you will be required to pay National Insurance Contributions (NICs) to the Department of Social Security. These payments build up your entitlement to certain state benefits, including the State Pension.

You pay Class 2 National Insurance contributions at a flat rate of £2.80 a week and can be paid either monthly by direct debit or by quarterly bill. If your earnings are below £5,965 per year (2015-16) you may not need to pay.

You may also need to pay Class 4 contributions depending on your profits. Class 4 National Insurance contributions are based on your profits for the year. You pay 9% on annual profits between £8,060 and £42,385 (2015-16) and 2% on any profit over that amount. Class 4 NI contributions are paid with your income tax payments.

VAT

If your turnover is above a certain level, (£82,000 per annum 2015-16) you must apply for value added tax (VAT) registration. This means you will be collecting VAT from your customers and paying it to HMRC, and this is set against the VAT you have paid out on your expenses. Quarterly VAT returns must be completed and sent to HMRC along with any payment due.

The VAT forms are simple and usually work in your favour. Although you must pay VAT on any income generated, you can claim back VAT paid on goods and services, including office supplies, vehicle servicing and fuel. Companies whose turnover is less than the VAT limit can still register voluntarily. Remember many food products are VAT exempt so consider carefully whether it is worth registering, if you are not at the VAT limit.

A VAT registration covers all the business activities of the registered person. This means you cannot hive off parts of your business so that you fall outside the VAT threshold. Partnerships are regarded as a single entity for VAT purposes. Limited companies are also regarded as individual entities. You will also be required to complete form VAT2 with the partnership details if you are registering a partnership for VAT purposes, although at the time of writing this form was not available to complete online.

Auditing

HMRC audit a small percentage of companies each year check for tax evasion. They have effective ways of tracking suspicious returns.

The auditing process is thorough and time-consuming because all receipts and invoices must be checked against the returns and shown to the investigating accountant. You may have to produce paperwork going back many years. Because of this, you may want to take out auditing insurance (see insurances on Page 31) to cover time and expense.

You will be expected to account for every single penny spent in relation to the business, and show each month's transactions in sufficient detail that your profit and loss, income and expenditure can be clearly calculated.

Banks

As a sole trader, your business is not legally separate from the self-employed person who is running it. Therefore it does not necessarily require a business account. It is not a legal requirement to run a separate bank account for your business though banks clearly would prefer that you do. Major banks are usually keen to get you on board for the future custom you may bring, but shop around until you find a bank that best suits your needs. By not using a business bank account, you may be able to save on bank charges that are usually applied to business accounts.

If you do retain your personal bank account, you must be able to distinguish your personal spending from that of your business for tax purposes. However there may be reasons why it could be better to open a separate business account.

- Some bank's terms and conditions for their personal bank accounts, may prevent it from being used for a business.
- If you are running more than one self-employed business you may prefer to have a separate account for each business though this is not a legal requirement.
- Bookkeeping is easier if all the transactions relating to your business are together and separate from your personal bank account. This gives you clarity when monitoring the account and will give some idea of the profit or loss being made.
- If you are using a different business name, and receive cheques in that name, it might not be possible to pay them into a personal bank account.
- You may wish to receive payments by credit card or debit card which are unlikely to be possible with a personal bank account.
- Business money can be left in the account for tax purposes to ensure it is there when required.

Note: It is not a specific legal requirement for a limited company to operate a business bank account, however not doing so can lead to potential legal and tax difficulties. It is advisable for a limited company to have a separate bank account.

Start-up Costs

Premises

You will want to give your company the best chance of surviving and thriving, so your premises might need to be flexible to give your business room to ebb and flow in it's early stages, when performance is difficult to predict. Your premises should reflect where your business currently stands and where you want it to go and it will affect how your business is perceived.

Working from your home is often the best option for a low cost way to set up your business and take it through the early stages, whilst building your client base and establishing yourself. Using your home will avoid any substantial initial layout for premises, but for some this might be impossible due to space, property restrictions or other personal considerations.

If you are going to be running your business from home, and you need regular deliveries, consider your neighbours. The local council or neighbours could take out an injunction against you if they feel it causes too much noise or inconvenience. Speak to your local council to see if you have to pay business rates on the part of your home you use for business.

If you're looking to find separate premises from your home there are a number of factors which you should consider for the best chance of success. Running your business from anywhere other than your home will incur the cost of premises. This can vary enormously from a few thousand pounds to tens of thousands a year.

While renting premises might seem like the only sensible option given your financial situation, you will not end up owning the property. Mortgage repayments are a major financial commitment but will generally be no more expensive than renting premises, and it will allow you to more easily make structural and/or cosmetic changes to suit your business.

If purchasing a property is not something you could consider, it may be worth discussing your options with commercial property holders like 'Swift Capital', who can buy premises on your behalf and rent them back to you. This gives you the option to retain the space without needing to own it. This involves making an agreement with the buyers establishing you as the preferred tenant.

For many people, running a business from home is often the best or only option. You might feel that operating from home might actually hold you back. Logistics, personal relationships, isolation and taking on staff, may all be factors affecting your decision on premises. Image is an important consideration and it plays a role when developing relationships with potential clients, suppliers, and even employees. If you want a prominent public presence, your home may not be the best place out of which to achieve this.

Leasing, building or buying premises as a start-up, may well be the least relevant options to begin with due to the considerable investment required but, when the business reaches the right stage further down the line, taking out a long-term lease or even buying your own premises may be the right option.

If you choose to rent a property for your business, you have some responsibilities by law - but most will depend on what it says in the lease. The Health and Safety Executive's 'Workplace health, safety and welfare: a short guide' has more details, particularly if you plan to have any staff. There is more on this subject later in this guide, in the section on Health and Safety.

Basic equipment

You will need to source a considerable amount of equipment (though you may have much of this already) and this may require an initial outlay to set you up. What you buy also depends on how big an operation you want to start.

All equipment costs, including consumables and utilities, count as expenses which you can claim against tax. Some items will be capital expenses and may form some of your start-up costs. You will also have ongoing costs. All of which will reduce your profit and therefore, your taxable income.

Capital items - ovens, fridges, computers, cars (purchased for your business), mixers, and other larger 'fixed' items can contribute towards your Annual Investment Allowance (AIA) which may be able to be claimed in full against tax.

Other costs include:
- General (cooking) equipment - utensils, tins, bowls, sugarcraft tools.
- Consumables - initial stock: cake boxes and boards, ingredients, colours, pastes.
- Office supplies - telephone, mobile, stationery equipment.

Additional non-essential equipment can be added over time. Many of these items will also be ongoing expenses to your business which can also be claimed against tax.

Ongoing Costs - Overheads, Variable and Fixed Costs

As with any business, less overheads means lower expenditure. Ongoing costs include all costs of your business - utilities, rental, consumables, equipment, insurance, repairs, petrol and even tax payments.

Choose suppliers carefully to make sure that you get the right product at the best price and that the delivery is frequent and reliable. In the food industry it is also important to know the traceability of your products. Know from where your products are sourced and be able to show evidence of this traceability.

Keep a record of the running costs for your business. Expenses can build up, make sure they add positively to the profitability of your business. Your spending will include many necessary costs, but ensure **all** spending is necessary, productive, and carefully considered for your business' ongoing and increasing profitability. All recorded costs can be set against tax.

Insurance

Protect your business so that it can keep working when you are unable. As a sole trader your business will come to a standstill unless you have staff or are able to make alternative arrangements should you have an accident, fall ill or even go on holiday.

If your livelihood depends upon your income, shop around for health and medical insurance tailored to small businesses with self-employed owners. Consider taking out disability insurance to cover you for time off through illness or injury. Check the qualifying period as some policies with lower premiums may not pay out until after an excess period of several months.

Check to see if subsidised insurance schemes are offered by your trade association are available - see page 34 for details of The British Sugarcraft Guild's insurance.

You may want to take out additional auditing insurance with your accountant. The work involved during an audit by HMRC is considerable and could become very expensive if you pay your accountant by the hour.

Business insurance

Your standard household insurance policy may not provide you with adequate cover for your business activities. Domestic insurance policies generally only cover very basic clerical and administration duties. Household insurance will be affected when you keep physical stock and/or money related to the business at home, or if you receive clients at your house. Any equipment bought for the purposes of work will not be covered and you risk your household policy being invalidated if you make a business related claim. Employee Liability Insurance will not be included in any household insurance policy.

Currently business insurance for the home cake decorator is optional. Employers liability insurance is a legal requirement if you have staff. It would be unwise to operate without at least some basic business insurance. Public and product liability is recommended.

There are many insurance schemes on the market for small businesses but it is worth shopping around and thinking carefully about exactly what you want to be covered.

You will need to choose what you require in your insurance cover:

- **Home insurance** - your private policy will not cover your home if you are using it for business purposes. You must notify your insurer that you intend running a business from home and separate insurance is required for the business.
- **Public liability** - cover for a business if a customer or member of the public was to suffer a loss or injury as a result of its business activities and if that person made a claim for compensation. The insurance covers the compensation payment plus any legal expenses.
- **Property owners liability** - cover that offers protection to the owner of a building or land, in case accidents or injury befall third parties, or visitors to your premises.
- **Employer liability** (a legal requirement if you employ one or more members of staff) - covers you as an employer, for the health and safety of your employees while they are at work. In the event your employees are injured or become ill at work, they may try to claim compensation from you if they believe you are responsible.
- **Product liability** - covers your business against claims made against your products. You are liable for harm caused by any unsafe product and you can be sued by anyone who is harmed, even if they didn't buy the product themselves. You can be sued for compensation for death or injury.
- **Goods in transit** - covers goods or products against loss or damage whilst in transit including (optional) storage during a journey. You can take this insurance out for goods being distributed in your own vehicle or by a third-party carrier, both domestically and abroad.
- **Property insurance** - covers a business premises against damage to the building from disasters such as fire, flood, theft etc.
- **Fixtures and fittings** - contents insurance covers your possessions, but you may want to take out insurance to cover fixed items such as shelving, kitchen units, carpet or flooring, counters, fixed display cases etc.
- **Contents of your premises** - covers the contents of your business premises against damage, destruction, loss or theft. This can

include cash if you hold it at your premises.

- **Stock cover** - covers stock on your premises. It is advisable to insure stock separately from your contents insurance. Stock value can run to thousands of pounds if damaged, destroyed or stolen.
- **Tools cover** - covers your tools and equipment for loss, damage or theft. If you store your tools overnight in a vehicle, you can get insurance to cover this circumstance as well. You can also get cover for your tools while they are in transit.
- **Your car** - covers a whole range of uses, such as travelling between different work locations, visiting customers or using your own vehicle to transport goods or employees. Anything, in fact, that is on behalf of the company. You will pay higher premiums for business insurance, but do not be tempted to stick with domestic-only cover. An insurer is unlikely to pay out any claims if it discovers the accident happened while you were using your vehicle for business.
- **Vehicle breakdown insurance** - vehicle breakdown cover is advisable to cover you in the event of a breakdown, if only to ensure that you are still able to continue to carry out your business. Some policies can also save you valuable money on repairs as a result of vehicle breakdowns.
- **Breakdown insurance** - 24 hour breakdown cover for your home and kitchen appliances is also something you may wish to consider. What happens to your business if a power failure prevents baking for example?
- **Personal insurance** - covers you if you suffered an accident and were admitted to hospital, or left permanently disabled. This may be vital if your household is dependent upon your business earnings.
- **Auding insurance** - an optional cover should you be required to carry out an audit in the case of financial investigation.

You may feel that not all these insurances are required. For example, if you never deliver cakes, "goods or equipment in transit" may not be necessary. If customers never visit your premises you may choose not to have property owners insurance. Think carefully about what you require and shop around.

Insurance through The British Sugarcraft Guild
Note: The following is correct at the time of writing, but this can change at any time.

For small businesses The British Sugarcraft Guild (BSG) offers insurance negotiated at favourable rates for members of the Guild who are pursuing sugarcraft as a part-time hobby, with a turnover of less than £8,500 per annum (2015-16). This is negotiated through ADS Insurance Brokers Limited.

This insurance is available to all BSG members through their branch or to individual members through the National Office or via their website at www.bsg.co.uk

The policy is an 'umbrella' cover, e.g. all members taking out the cover under the one policy. The insurance year runs from 1st May to 30th April and the minimum insurance period is one year. You can join the BSG at any time, but the premium and renewal period remains the same.

There are different levels of insurance available, depending on the cover required and prices range from £17.00 to £91.10 (2015-2016).

Amount of cover	2 million	5 million
Public & Products - Liability only	£17.00	£27.50
Public & Products - plus all risks cake cover	£70.00	£80.50
Public & Products - plus all risks cake cover and money cover	£80.60	£91.10

This table is for information purposes only. For full information including limitations to this cover you should contact The British Sugarcraft Guild's National Office.

The British Sugarcraft Guild's package of Public/Product Liability Insurance includes:

I) Public Liability
2) Products Liability
3) Indemnity Limits
4) Additional Covers

Exclusions include:

a) Members who turnover more than £8,500 per annum (2015-2016) from their sugarcraft activities.
b) Insurance is provided for UK members only
c) Products Liability in respect of the USA and Canada.
d) Loss or damage to the cake unless the All Risk option has been requested.
e) Losses arising out of the use of a motor vehicle, including delivery.

Optional extras include:

All Risk cover, to your cakes/equipment
Money cover, to cover loss of money

Pensions

Although putting aside money for the future may be hard for you right now, a pension plan is well worth considering. This is not just for the financial security it will offer you when you retire. Investing in a pension scheme can have tax benefits too.

Everyone in the UK can get a basic state pension if they have built up sufficient National Insurance contributions over at least a quarter of their working life, but only those who have paid NI contributions for nine-tenths of their working lives will be entitled to the full state pension. It is therefore recommended that self-employed people make further pension arrangements.

Sole traders can contribute to a private pension scheme though this is optional. There are a number of pension schemes on the market specifically designed for self-employed people. Many of these allow you options to pay a lump sum, take a break from payments or even make withdrawals.

Loans

Before you start looking for business start-up funding, figure out exactly how much money you need to start and write your business plan. There are different ways to get the money you need for starting a business from home.

Business loans

There are several ways to take out a loan:

- **Bank loans**
  Getting a bank loan will require repaying the loan with interest (you will need to have good enough credit to obtain the loan in the first place).
- **Government loans**
  These are another possibility and should be looked into when looking for business start-up funding. Different levels of government have loans for initial home business start-up money.
- **Payday loans**
  If you only need a small amount of money for starting a business from home, you could explore the payday loan option. With payday loans, as with any other type of loan. You will have to pay interest (at possibly highly inflated rates) along with the loan, so study your options carefully.
- **Business grants**
  This may be worth a try to get free money. The government will, in some cases, offer business start-up funding to those people who wish to open a business. As a grant, this is money you do not have to repay. There are restrictions and limitations on some business grants so you really will not know until you try. Research different government grant agencies and see what they have to offer you.
- **Business credit cards or investors**
  Business credit cards with a high limit may provide your needs to fund your start-up business. There are many of these types of business credit cards that you can apply for and get to get your home business up and running.

If you're still struggling to find funding you could look for private investors who are willing to back your new start-up business.

Try to save up as much as possible before you open your home based business. Putting something into savings, however small, on an ongoing basis, will give you something to reinvest into your business in the future, and is a habit worth learning to retain a protective financial buffer.

Exploring the ideas above for funding to start your business from home will eventually help you find which path to take to get the capital you need to get started.

Staff

You may choose to employ staff. Staff can account for a large percentage of a business' turnover. You will need to weigh up the cost of labour against the increased profits generated.

There are no restrictions on staff numbers but if you employ staff you will be required to deduct PAYE tax from wages and pay it to the HMRC each month. You will also need to complete PAYE paperwork for your employees and a PAYE annual return each year. The relevant paperwork requires completion when a staff member leaves your employment.

As an employer you will also be responsible for your employees' Class 1 National Insurance contributions and your employer contributions calculated as a percentage of an employee's wage. You will also need to consider employment terms and contract as well as statutory sick pay, equal opportunities and health and safety conditions.

Health and safety for staff

If you decide to employ people to help you run your business, you are responsible for their health and safety. This includes any contract and freelance workers. You are also responsible for any visitors to your premises such as customers, suppliers and the general public.

The Health and Safety at Work Act 1974 is the primary legislation covering work-related health and safety in the United Kingdom. It sets out your employers' responsibilities for health and safety at work.

The Health and Safety Executive is responsible for enforcing health and safety at work and before you employ staff, you should carry out a thorough assessment of the health and safety risks of your business. If you have more than five staff members, you must provide written evidence of your health and safety policy and make sure the employees are aware of it. Make sure all your staff comply with health and safety procedures to prevent accidents. If an accident does occur, you are legally required to record and report it.

Accounts and Record Keeping

It is important that you set up a system for keeping your financial records, which includes maintaining all your business income and expenses. This is vital for tax purposes but is also beneficial to help you stay on top of your finances.

If you're setting up as a sole trader rather than as a company with employees, then your bookkeeping can be kept to a minimum. You will have to keep track of monthly income and expenditure.

You could manage your accounts by hand, but it is much more time efficient to use a computer. A spreadsheet containing income, expenditure and VAT (if you're VAT-registered) will suffice although you may choose to use an accounts package which links to HMRC to enable direct PAYE and other tax payments.

It is essential that you keep track of all invoices (along with the dates they were issued and the dates they were paid) and all receipts for work-related transactions.

If you work from home, some proportion of your household expenditure on things like rent, telephone bills, heating and electricity bills may be applied to your business. This can be set against your business and may be tax-deductible.

If you keep all this information in order you will have all you need to fill in your Self Assessment Tax Return each year. It need not be an arduous process and it should be possible to maintain your books with just as a couple of hours work each month.

The prospect of dealing with HMRC can seem quite frightening, but they aim to help businesses and individuals manage their accounts as effectively as possible. They have teams of advisors on hand to help out anyone who might get into difficulties.

Getting things started

Before you even launch your own business, talk to the local HMRC. Make an appointment and explain your business plan. Ask them exactly what you need and they will provide you with advice, leaflets and forms - such as VAT registration - for you to complete before you begin trading.

If you have the necessary information at the start, it will make your bookkeeping process much easier. It will give you confidence at the beginning if you have contact with the local offices to call whenever you have any queries.

Good bookkeeping

Accountants' bills are high so if you are going to use one, maintain good bookkeeping methods to save you money. Try not to let paperwork, particularly accounts, build up, unchecked.

Follow a few basic guidelines to help you keep costs down:
- **Keep all paperwork.**
  Keep a record of everything, bank statements, credit card slips, bills, invoices and payment receipts.

- **Do regular checks.**
  At least twice a year, or quarterly if possible, visit, check and update your records. Check payments and credits against your bank or credit card statements. Make sure you remained tuned to how your money is performing for you. We have all heard the stories of bank errors, do not let them go unchecked.
- **Write it all down.**
  Enter everything into a computer system or book. Use numbering to keep track of invoices, payment receipts and payments in. This tedious paperwork will cost you dearly if done by an accountant and much of this is straightforward to do yourself. If you do not have the time or inclination, then try to find a bookkeeper who will charge a lower rate than that of an accountant.
- **Computerise where possible.**
  Most accountants will expect to receive a set of accounts on a computer. Some accountants will only use certain software so check what they use, and that it is compatible with your system. HMRC will take computerised tax forms too so, if you are not using an accountant, this will help with dealing directly with them.
- **Don't forget to save.**
  Try to put aside a quarter of every payment you receive. This will give you a fund for the tax bill. In reality you probably will not maintain this but you will have to budget for the tax bill. You will find it easier to do if, from an early stage you put aside a regular saving towards such payments. You could consider using a monthly direct debit to pay into a savings account for tax purposes.

Keeping business records

Minimum periods exist for keeping records. six years for VAT and five years from the latest date for filing your Self Assessment return. You can keep your records in paper or electronic format.

You must keep:
- Annual accounts, including profit and loss accounts.
- Bank statements and paying-in slips.
- Cash books and other account books.
- Orders and delivery notes.

- Purchase and sales books.
- Records of daily takings such as till rolls.
- Relevant business correspondence.

You must keep the following VAT records:
- Records of all the goods and services you buy or sell.
- Copies of all sales invoices you issue.
- All purchase invoices for items you buy.
- All credit notes and debit notes you receive.
- Copies of all credit notes and debit notes you issue.
- Any self-billing agreements you make as a supplier.
- Copies of self-billing agreements you make as a customer and name, address and VAT registration number of the supplier.
- Records of any goods you give away or take from stock for your private use including rate and amount of VAT.
- Records of any goods or services bought for which you cannot reclaim the VAT.
- Any documents dealing with special VAT treatment.
- Records of any goods you export.
- Records of any taxable self-supplies you make, for example, if you provide a product or service to a family member which would be subject to VAT you must keep record of it.
- Any adjustments such as corrections to your accounts or amended VAT invoices.
- The gross amount of each payment you make to a sub-contractor, excluding VAT.
- The amount of any deduction you made from a payment before you gave it to the subcontractor.
- If you made a deduction, the amount of any material costs, excluding VAT.

Pricing structure

Knowing what to charge for your work can be quite a daunting area for the new business owner. You need to think about the value of what you do.

If you have previously been employed, your employer was the one who knew the price to charge for services, and how much your contribution was worth to them.

People will often call a business up and ask 'what do you charge?' It may be a straightforward question, but the answer is not so simple.

Cake decorators will charge enormously different rates. We all have different skill levels and we tackle different types of cake projects. We also have different expectations of our earnings and different sets of overheads to cover.

Hence, it can be hard to have a set rate. Clients will however, often need a ball park figure, so it is wise to do some research into how much you are going to charge and what your market can bear.

Calculating an hourly rate

You first need to determine what it will cost to maintain your ongoing business. You will need to charge for the actual costs of each cake order. Then, as you are selling time and knowledge as part of your service you will need to calculate this element as part of your costs.

Do not underestimate the full costs of starting up and maintaining a business. Remember to include all your costs, including ongoing expenses and new investments in tools and equipment, premises, expansion etc.

You cannot simply charge by the hour for the time it takes you to complete one cake order. A lot of your time will be used running parts of the business which involve no cake at all.

It takes you time to bake a cake and decorate it and you must charge for this time accordingly. But you also need to spend time shopping, doing the accounts, having phone conversations with clients or the bank manager. All these elements take up valuable business time and need to be accommodated.

Your business has many ongoing costs which need accounting for when fixing a pricing structure. These include:
* Ongoing recurring expenses including rental or mortgage, phone and utility bills, postage, broadband and web hosting, printing and copying, office supplies, memberships, subscriptions, groceries, other consumables (cake boxes and boards), travel

and professional services such as accountancy.

- Maintaining office and kitchen equipment, furniture, machinery, kitchen tools, camera, computer purchases and upgrades, filing cabinets, a desk and so on.
- Tax. You are responsible for your own tax affairs and you must account for these payments.
- Benefits you may have to fund like pensions, holiday pay and insurances.

By adding these items together you will arrive at a figure that represents the cost of running your business each year. What you charge needs to cover these costs and still achieve the required profit margin to give you an income relevant to your skill and enough for you to live on. Plan to earn something close to what you may get in full-time employment, otherwise there is not much point in doing it!

You need to work out what is your billable time. Work out how many hours you will be able to, and want to work. This needs to take account of all the holiday time, sick days, days without work and unpaid work like personal administration and marketing that you will not be able to charge directly for.

Try to decide on a realistic number of hours you can expect to charge for over one year. Let us start with $5\frac{1}{2}$ hours a day for 52 weeks, that is nearly 27 hours a week.

The time will need to be redistributed if you take holidays or are sick. So let's say you want to work for 48 weeks of the year to give you four weeks holiday. If you still want to work 1,440 hours per year, you will now need to work six hours per day to allow for the holiday time.

So, you are able to work for six hours per day for five days per week, that is 30 hours per week for 48 weeks a year. To calculate the number of hours you will work over the year, multiply 30 hours per week by 48 weeks per year which will give you 1,440 hours per year.

Divide your total cost of running the business for one year, by the number of paid hours you aim to work, to give you an hourly rate to cover your costs. So if the business costs you £7,000 per year to run, and you work 1,400 hours, your minimum hourly cost is £5 per hour. This will cover your running costs but leave nothing to take home!

If you want to earn, for example, £14,000 per year, your business will need an income of £21,000 (£7,000 + £14,000).

Divide £21,000 by 1,400 (the number of hours) to give you an hourly rate.

You will need to charge £15 per hour to cover your costs and give you the profit margin for your chosen income.

The table below illustrates this calculation.

My business will cost me £7,000 per year in expenses.	
.I want to earn £14,000 profit per year (£1,166 pcm).	
So the business needs an annual turnover of £21,000 to survive.	
How many weeks per year do I want to work? (52 minus 4 weeks holiday)	**48 weeks per year**
How many hours per week can I work? (6 hours per day over 5 days)	**30 Hours per week**
How many hours over 12 months? (30 x 48)	**1,440 hours per year**
£21,000 1,440 hours to give my hourly rate	**£14.58**
This is a basic example of how to work out a rate that is right for you. It does not take into account individual circumstances and things like sickness or mechanical breakdown.	

It is worth asking around to see if this is realistic. If it appears that you are being a bit optimistic, you may have to revisit your personal income expectations, look at ways of cutting costs, or think again about the type of work you are pursuing. You can raise your hourly rate if it seems a little too low. Charging too little can give the perception of a lower quality product or service.

Pricing cakes is particularly difficult and your calculations to set an hourly rate, will become an integral part of your individual cake order calculations.

Chapter 12 covers how to calculate cake costs including ingredients, boxes, boards etc., while not forgetting your hourly rate. We also cover the use of cake calculating apps like The Cake Makery's Cost-a-Cake Pro, which is designed to provide fast results if you are providing prices to customers on a regular basis.

Making a profit

Those going into a new business should be prepared not to make an immediate profit. You need patience, and acceptance that you may not make much money at the early stages of a new business. You may feel the effort and money being put in is not giving the expected reward, and this is to be expected in the early months and even years.

You may have to accept the fact that in the beginning, it will take much of your energy, money and hours, reinvesting hard earned money, for machinery and equipment and developing the business. This will reduce any immediate profit in the early stages but will hopefully build a solid base on which to grow your business. Do not expect large and immediate returns. You need to be prepared to be in it for the long haul to reap the fullest benefits.

Chapter 3

Marketing, Promotion & Advertising

You will not sell anything if no one knows who you are! You need to tell your target market about your business. Take every available opportunity to meet people, nurture potential clients and create interest in your business. The amount of marketing you do it is entirely up to you.

General guidelines recommend that a business' marketing costs should be 1 to 10% of annual sales. Adjust upward (to as much as 20-30% if you can) if you are launching a new business or adjust downward if you are continuing a well known operation.

The advantage of using sales as your basis to calculate advertising and marketing spend is that if you experience a slow period, it will automatically reflect in your marketing budget. Work out exactly how much you can realistically afford to invest in advertising.

Attracting new customers is pointless if you are unable to keep up your mortgage payments or pay your phone bill. If you advertise in more than one way, monitor the business generated from each source so that you can ensure your money in being spent in the most effective way.

As a business you must decide which media to use to market your product. Advertising has traditionally been through print advertisements, radio and television commercials, direct mail/leaflet campaigns, telephone book ads and attendance at trade shows and exhibitions.

The Internet means there are numerous other forms of marketing available to you, much of which is more affordable. Running your own website is almost essential these days. Marketing through social media sites like Facebook or Twitter is very effective, economical, and accessible to a large proportion of the population. Using blogs and video presentations on sites like YouTube, are also good ways to spread the news of who you are and what you do.

Getting a Portfolio Together

A portfolio is invaluable when discussing orders with clients and to use at any opportunity to shout about your business. It is also your record of all you have done. It will show you how far you have come, but make sure you keep up-to-date and current images in any portfolio you use for sales and customer consultations.

The use of images of cakes you produce will soon fill a portfolio but do not forget to include other items of interest. If you manage to create a cake that is published in the local paper for example, include that article, it creates a good impression of your business. Include items even if they are not whole cakes. On occasions you may be asked to make cake toppers and models or flower sprays, these are all just as valuable in a portfolio, to show off your skill and adaptability.

You may choose to split your folios into different categories. It can be helpful, if you have many pictures, to create a folio of wedding cakes, separate from birthday cakes, other occasion cakes and models etc. but this is up to you. A customer coming to you for a wedding cake consultation may not wish to wade through your portfolio of children's party cakes and models to find your wedding cake photos.

Photography

The quality of the photographs you use in your portfolio will have an effect on your customers. If your photos are small, out of focus and generally not of a good standard, this will reflect on you. Are your cakes going to be of a similarly poor quality? If you are not a good photographer it is worth considering paying someone initially to get some good photographs of your work.

Ultimately it might be worth considering spending time and money on learning how to take reasonable photographs yourself, as it is expensive to have to book a professional photographer every time you need new images.

Your photographs can be easily enhanced using good lighting and wallpaper backdrops that you could obtain quite cheaply to enhance your pictures. Avoid cluttered kitchen surfaces in the background and edit final pictures before selecting only the best.

Make sure your portfolio is also presentable. An envelope or a few plastic sleeves in a ring binder, containing a few of your latest snaps is not professional. Use a clean and clearly presented A4 portfolio, which can be easily purchased though most stationers. This gives you the opportunity to include clear title pages giving your details.

Free Marketing

Exploit all the free market information available, and market like mad. You need to get the word out, so network. Start by telling your friends and family about your new business, encouraging them to pass on a good word for you. Let everyone you know what it is you are up to. Tell any groups, PTA, clubs, neighbours, etc. Word of mouth is your most valuable form of promotion when starting out.

Try to spot new market trends so that you can exploit them before someone else does. Create a network of business allies, this could provide you with a constant stream of orders. Find, and look after profitable business customers as they will hopefully talk about you. Get in magazines and on TV for free. Get your cakes in high street shop windows for free.

Business Cards

Carry business cards with you at all times. You never know when a marketing or business opportunity might arise. There are many good deals to be found for the printing of business cards, so it is worth shopping around.

Self Promotion

If you want more business, make sure your cakes are better or more original than the local competition including local bakers. Aim to take business away from your competitors. Get all those friends who are willing to pay for your cakes to help spread word of your business. You may even find them willing to distribute flyers and even discount coupons for your business!

Approach local cake and coffee shops about taking samples and selling your goods. Although many may refuse, just one or two will spread knowledge of you and give your business a tremendous boost. Handing out free samples, instead of spending money on fancy advertising, will get your cakes out there and noticed.

Contact local wedding planners to show your wedding cakes. A well made wedding cake can really get you noticed with wedding planners. Planners may get you referrals to other party organisers as well as event managers.

Sponsoring a local event or church fundraising activity creates great exposure. Free samples at this type of event may really get you noticed. You can rent a table/stall at a local fair, school fête or market, attend industry trade shows, or host your own event.

Keep the interest going. You may be able to offer a large cake for a local children's hospice or old people's home for example. The cake could be donated or raffled and the proceeds given to a charity, this generates publicity and may even get your business recognition in the local papers.

Provide raffle prizes to local events (well labelled of course!), or a promised cake for a promises auction. This may get your name in the programme for the event and more free publicity. A little time well spent may generate great publicity, which is priceless!

Turn your portfolio into a selling machine. Make sure it contains all you wish to shout about and not what you don't!

Advertising

Advertise without breaking the bank whenever you can. Put up flyers in local shops, have friends post reviews of your business and put signs in your car window. Research carefully for profitable advertising that is cost effective.

Advertising can be in many forms, from classified adverts in magazines, to web advertising.

Here is a selection:
- Local newspapers.
- Local magazines.
- Cake directory magazines.
- Wedding & bridal magazines.
- Parish magazines.
- Local event publications.
- Supermarket advert boards.
- Local schools (book bags).
- Wedding supplier services.
- Venue publicity material.
- Wedding fair publicity material.
- Yell and Thompson Local.
- Vehicle signage.

- Flyers (door-to-door or as inserts).
- Local shop windows.
- Facebook and Google.

Think carefully about where and how your advertising budget can be spent most effectively. There are numerous ways to advertise if you are willing to pay and you may find after your first advert you get a raft of calls from other publications wanting you to spend your money with them! Choose wisely!

Printed flyers can be distributed locally via leaflet drops, or if you have the budget, inserted into local papers. They can also be left in local places like shops, pubs, restaurants, hairdressers etc.

Sites like Guides for Brides, The National Wedding Guide and Hitched, allow you to pay for an account that lets you set up a profile. They are all a little different, but with some you can offer promotions to potential customers, update your portfolio pictures, and company information and even have your customers post reviews of your products. Some also offer printed media to accompany your web advert, which will further your reach.

It is worth spending a little time doing some local and Internet research for your region as your cake making business might be fairly local, so it may not be the best use of your hard earned cash to blow it on a glossy advert in a national magazine. However if you regularly drive around your neighbourhood, delivering cakes, or children to school, advertising on your car could be very profitable.

Think about coinciding magazine advertising with bridal and wedding fairs or other special occasions. Bear in mind that many publications have long lead times so you may have to plan your advertising many months in advance of publication.

Do not forget that there are many local magazines and publications. Church groups, sports groups and local communities usually have their own publications. Enquire about advertising rates as these are often much cheaper than glossy magazines and will reach a very local target market. Many of these publications will also promote local events for free if you are holding a local cake demonstration and sale for example.

Some methods of advertising may not work for you. In order for you to not waste your precious budget, you should set aside a little time to track your advertising.

Offline advertising is much harder to gauge as you will never know exactly how many people saw it. You should ask everyone who contacts you, where they heard about you, or offer a unique promotion that allows you to know where they came from without asking.

Online advertising is much easier, as the digital world tracks everything. You can find out how many views your advert receives, how many people click it, and if that click generates an order.

Keeping track of your statistics is extremely useful if your budget is very small, and you want to maximise the results.

Brochures and Flyers

A simply produced flyer, (but at the very least your business card) is invaluable. Hand them to anyone who asks, and keep them on you at all times.

You can take more time to develop brochures or flyers when you can sensibly assess the need. Often online promotion is more effective, unless you are attending many events where printed promotional material can be more useful. It is possible to spend lots on design and print for only a very small return.

Be careful where you use leaflets and brochures as you could find yourself distributing hundreds of beautifully printed brochures where an A5 leaflet or DL flyer would have served the purpose much more economically.

Sometimes a venue which you have supplied to may approach you for inclusion in their promotion literature for their wedding services. Again, take care to consider this very carefully. Look at costs against longevity - some brochures are produced annually, but others are bi-annual giving you a longer presence in their literature. And while some may be economically priced, others can be very expensive! It is only one venue, so how many cakes would you need to make, to cover the cost of the advertising taken in their annual or bi-annual brochure?

Venues, churches, schools, and village halls may allow you to leave some of your leaflets out for potential customers to pick up. Local events may also be happy to support you by handing out leaflets. A school fund-raiser, like a summer fair, may be an ideal place to catch some local custom by handing out a few flyers.

Labels and Stickers

Stickers for your cake boxes and labels on all the products you produce are a great way to advertise. Make sure they carry your logo and contact details. You can also use these labels on any letters and parcels.

Wedding Fairs and Exhibitions

Wedding fairs and exhibitions can be very useful but may also be very time consuming, and the cost, both of booking and your preparation, can be quite high. Check to see which other traders will be present. Think about whether the effort is worth it for the potential reward. Wedding fairs and exhibitions require you to take time out from your fee-paying business to prepare for, and attend the event.

You will probably need to bake cake samples and create several display cakes. You will also need literature, flyers and at the very least, business cards to hand out. You will need an up to date appointments diary to take bookings and a pricing structure which is simple and easy to use on the day.

Apps like Cost-a-Cake Pro can prove invaluable for times like these when potential customers want up front answers. Along with your portfolio, you will also need to be armed with plenty of information, leaflets and business cards.

Some events and wedding fairs, offer a 'bag' service. A 'goodie bag' is handed to every bride attending the event, and you may be able to have your literature included in these bags whilst not actually attending the event in person. This means that every bride will take home information about the services you offer. As is the case with any advertising like this, there can be a large outlay for a very small return so study the figures carefully before committing.

In my experience bridal and wedding fairs or exhibitions (or their goodie bags) rarely prove worthwhile promotional tools. They may generate new business but this must be measured against the time and money invested in attending.

These events could easily use up a large portion of your advertising budget. If however, an event is run by (and at) a venue you regularly attend for your clients, you may find you are at a greater advantage to pick up new business.

Branching Out

Offering related products as well as cakes may make business more viable. Cake related items which can be sent mail-order may boost your business, but bear in mind any additional work load as well as any new costs to the business.

Local Television and Radio

Radio and television is an ideal way to reach potential customers. Initially the expense may be outside most budgets, but it may be worth considering as your business becomes more established. It may be possible to get some free airtime on local radio stations. If a broadcaster is presented with an interesting local feature, with something different to offer, there may be opportunities available that could be very beneficial to your business.

Getting Online - Your Website

A website is almost essential for you if you're working from home as you don't have a shop window. Get your portfolio online. A well designed and easily navigable website can reach a wide audience 24 hours a day.

Make sure it remains up-to-date, not just the information but also with current images showing modern trends. You could have reviews, include a blog or other cake-related content to keep your visitors coming back.

Websites can vary in cost, but you can do a basic one with a simple package quite cheaply and this can give you a domain name, and the possibility of an online shop.

You can put your whole portfolio online, adding to it when you have new photos. When you are starting out with a new website, you will have to think carefully about what content you want to display. You will have to write all the text and select all the photos for your site!

The more professional-looking the website appears, the more likely consumers are to buy from you. You need to differentiate yourself from the competition, or you risk undermining the quality of your products. Your customers will be less inclined to spend if your website lets you down.

If you have something that looks like it has been photographed in your kitchen, this is going to let you down on your website. If it looks like it could be featured in a magazine, people will trust the site. People are used to looking at magazine-quality pictures. The moment someone has to decipher what you are photographing, that's when people will lose trust.

Ask yourself what your business will be selling – is it bespoke cakes, pre-designed off-the-shelf cakes, or will there be other products too? These type of questions are very important as they determine the type of website that you need to create.

A portfolio site does not require any highly technical skills to build as the pages are usually just text and photos. You would display information about your business, your contact details, and a gallery of your work. If you want people to be able to buy and pay online, you will need e-commerce capabilities.

There are different ways you can approach getting a website built. You need to think about the amount of knowledge and time you have to set up and run your website. Decide if you can manage this yourself, or if you need external help.

If you generate your own website make sure it is mobile and tablet friendly. This means that your website should be responsive and scale to fit any device that it is viewed on.

70% of The Cake Makery website visitors access our website via a tablet or mobile phone. Compare this to 26% just 2 years ago, and you can see why this is now such an important consideration. Google's latest policy is to promote mobile friendly websites first.

It takes a lot of time to create the content, design the look & feel, and build the pages for your website. It will take a lot of time away from making cakes if you do it yourself. Getting someone else to do this for you will give you that time back, but cost you money.

A professional website that is created for you by a web development company can be expensive but it is worth spending the money if you can. They will design and build your complete website from scratch, which means you can have exactly what you want!

Managing the content yourself once the site is online is often quicker and costs you nothing if you do it yourself. A third party company may not be available right away.

Creating an e-commerce site is a lot more work! It is far more technically complex, due to requiring a database to store your product information, a shopping cart system, different payment methods and the ability to store your customers data securely. We would advise against you doing this yourself!

However, there are lots of companies who can provide this facility for you! Bigcommerce.com is a good place to start if you are looking to run an online shop. They have payments set up automatically with PayPal and lots of ready made templates that you can easily convert to your content with little or no technical knowledge.

They provide you with a system that allows you to quickly add new products, manage your customers and keep your website up to date. You can be up and running in just a few weeks with this type of shop, and the initial outlay is low, however you will have to pay them an ongoing monthly fee to keep your website online.

Watermarked images

Consider placing a copyright watermark on all your images for your protection. Once your images are on the Internet, who knows where they might end up!

Marking your images will identify them as yours, and protect your copyright of a cake design while providing you with free exposure if it is shared online! This can be very expensive unless you are able to apply this to your images yourself before uploading to the website.

Disclaimer

If you do generate a website for use by potential customers, where anyone in the world can see your work, consider a disclaimer for the website. This can be invaluable in protecting you and your business.

Example Website Disclaimer

Please read this disclaimer in full before you use this website. Using the website implies that you accept the terms of this disclaimer.

1. Use of the website

Material on this website cannot be republished online or offline without our permission. However you are permitted to use our website for your own purposes, to print or download material from our website provided that you do not modify any content without our written permission.

Copyright on all materials on this website are owned by us or our licensor and must not be reproduced without our prior written consent.

2. Conduct of visitors to the website

With the exception of personally identifiable information, any material you send or post to our website shall be considered non-proprietary and not confidential. Unless you advise to the contrary we will therefore be free to copy, disclose, distribute, incorporate and otherwise use such material for any purpose.

When using this website you shall not post or send any material for which you have not obtained all necessary consents, is discriminatory, obscene, pornographic, defamatory, liable to incite racial hatred, in breach of confidentiality or privacy, which may cause annoyance or inconvenience to others, which encourages or constitutes conduct that would be deemed a criminal offence, give rise to a civil liability, or otherwise is contrary to the law in the United Kingdom.

3. Set-up time

We endeavour to take all reasonable steps to ensure that our website is available 24 hours every day, 365 days per year. However, websites do sometimes encounter downtime due to server and, other technical issues. Therefore we will not be liable if this website is unavailable at any time.

4. Links to and from other websites

Any links to third party websites located on this website are provided for your convenience only. We have not reviewed each third party website and have no responsibility for such third party websites or their content.

If you would like to link to this website, you may only do so on the basis that you link to, but do not replicate, any page on this website and you do not in any way imply that we are endorsing any services or products unless this has been specifically agreed with us in writing.

If you link to our website in breach of the above, you shall fully indemnify us for any loss or damage suffered as a result of your actions.

5. Exclusion of liabilities

We take all reasonable steps to ensure that the information on this website is correct. However, we do not guarantee the correctness or completeness of material on this website. Neither we nor any other party (whether or not involved in producing, maintaining or delivering this website), shall be liable or responsible for any kind of loss or damage that may result to you or a third party as a result of your or their use of our website. This exclusion shall include servicing or repair costs and, without limitation, any other direct, indirect or consequential loss.

6. Law and jurisdiction

This Legal Notice shall be governed by and construed in accordance with English law. Any dispute(s) arising in connection with this Legal Notice are subject to the exclusive jurisdiction of England and Wales.

Getting Online –
Advertising your Website

Google AdWords is an online advertising service. It enables you to compete to display adverts on Google. There is a charge for the service. Based in part on keywords, your advert will show up when users search for keywords you have paid for.

To get your business at the very top of Google's search results, you can use Google AdWords: You choose keywords like flowers, cakes, chocolate or Surrey, and every time someone enters those search terms, your web link may appear at the top of the search results as a sponsored link.

Target the effort - Google will also help you spend your advertising budget wisely by targeting your adverts to your chosen demographic, and ensure that your adverts are only seen locally.

Once your advert has been running a few days, you can track the performance and tweak it accordingly.

You can also choose to place your adverts on similar websites that are signed up to the **Google AdSense** programme.

Facebook Adverts: You can purchase adverts that will appear on targeted News Feeds of potential new customers. Facebook is a good way to advertise as you can control the amount you spend per advert, or per day and you can track how many people have clicked through to your website.

LinkedIn is another good way to get your personal profile out there, make sure you fill in all the details and use their forums and notice boards to get yourself noticed.

Twitter: 651 million people use Twitter, so this is another great way to let people know who you are, tweet often about what you are up to, and follow lots of other cake-related people to build your own following for free.

Google Plus: If you have content to share, this is a good place to start. It includes Google groups, these are well used, and great for group discussion and publicity. There are lots of cake forums in here for fun chats with other cakers!

Cross Linking: This is designed to build traffic and increase your ranking on search engines. It relies on two websites agreeing to a link to the other site. It always helps to have as many links back into your website as possible, its all free publicity. It is also a good way of initially getting yourself indexed by search engines who value these links, as they are from relevant sites, with related content.

Promotional material: Display your web address on everything! The website is the first place most people will visit to find out more about your business.

We have given you a really brief outline, of how to get your business online and promote it. It is a huge, mind-boggling area that would take a whole book to cover completely. However, we hope to have given you a few pointers to get you started.

Getting Online - Your Facebook Page

Starting a business page on Facebook is different to your personal page, and is run as a separate entity. You must have a personal page in order to create a business page.

You can launch a Facebook page for your business without needing a website. If you are a brand new business, you should make this a priority as it costs you nothing and allows you to shout about yourself and post your precious portfolio! To build your audience you can invite your friends and family to like your new page, this will get the ball rolling and start to make you look popular.

If you have the budget, you can use Facebook advertising to attract new likes, by targeting people local to you. Your advert can encourage them to 'like' your page, so they will see some of the posts that you make going forward.

Facebook uses an algorithm to determine who sees your status updates. This means that not all of your posts will be seen by every person who likes your page. This is called 'reach'.

If you want to expand your reach, you must pay attention to what you are posting, the time of day that you are posting, and how many people interact with your posts.

This information is available via the Insights tab, and will allow you to track your followers' behaviour so that you can tweak your posts for maximum performance. We would advise that you make at least one status update each day.

Keep your followers up to date with what you are working on, share your photos, and try to post more if you possibly can. Remember though – quality is far more important that quantity.

Post daily

Keep your followers up to date with what you are working on.

Share

If you do not have fresh content of your own, share content from others that is cake related. In our experience we have found that people love to share photos of great cakes, recipes, tips and ideas. So sharing something that already seems popular, can increase your popularity too, which in turn, increases your reach.

Post lots of pictures

Post lots of pictures of your cakes, but do not forget to watermark the images with your copyright!

Great cake photos will get shared across people's news feeds. This means that someone who likes your page has just advertised your business to ALL of their friends. If one of their friends shares it, it then gets seen by their friends and so on, so you can quickly build a following if you get lucky.

Pay attention to Insights

Pay attention to Insights – this has already been mentioned, but this data is so valuable. It will tell you a lot about your followers, and there is a huge amount of free data available that tells you how well your Facebook page is performing. You can see how many people your messages are reaching, and which posts performed the best.

Use this information to give your fans the content they want to see. You can note the times they are around to see it, so you can adjust your posting habits to maximise reach and keep your followers coming back.

Keep Selling your Business

Constantly talk about your business at every opportunity and get as many friends and family as possible to do the same.

Use the Internet to post new photographs and video of cakes or products being made, on sites like You Tube. The more exposure you get, the better.

The best advice though, is to stay abreast of developments in the industry. Keep your cake designs on trend.

Trends, technologies and materials are constantly evolving, and staying aware of developments could mean the difference between getting a client or not.

Chapter 4

Premises

Homeowner Restrictions

You will need to check if business rates are payable on your property. Running a business from your home might affect the type of rates you pay. It will depend upon whether the part of your property you use for business is also used for domestic purposes.

For example, if you use a spare room or your kitchen for your work it is unlikely that you will pay business rates. But if you use an adapted garden shed or outbuilding for your business you may incur business rates.

The use of a domestic premises for business purposes may be construed as a change of use. It may be wise to seek the advise of the council's Planning Department. This may also affect your home insurance cover so check with your insurers.

Planning Permission

If you are proposing selecting a separate premises from home for your business, you will need to check that you will be able to get the necessary planning permission to run your food business. This will also apply if you wish to extend your home. If planning permission does not already exist, you will need to submit a planning application for building work with business use or for change of use of the premises.

Check with the Building Control Officer (also known as Building Control Surveyor) at your local borough council, if you need to carry out any construction work or alterations. The Building Control Officer will check if building regulation consent is required. They will also ensure any works carried out are done so in accordance with buildings regulations.

Another thing to bear in mind is whether your business is likely to cause any disturbance to your neighbours. Deliveries, visiting customers and noise, may all be considered a nuisance to your neighbours but if you keep them informed of what your plans are, they will be more likely to be supportive. You can discuss ways of easing any potential problems.

Mortgage

If you have a mortgage on your property, you must contact your lender to talk to them about your intentions. This applies to anyone who holds a financial interest in your home. Make sure you notify them of your intentions and ask them to acknowledge this and confirm their approval in writing. If you are using part of your house for business it is still wise to tell your mortgage lender (mortgagor). It will not normally make any difference but as the lender has an interest in your property, they should be informed of what it is being used for.

Beyond this, you are entitled to claim a suitable proportion of your mortgage interest payments against your tax. You cannot claim capital i.e. if you have already paid off, or do not have a mortgage. Putting a 'use of home' cost against tax is the easiest way to account for this without incurring complications if for example, your business was paying, and therefore becoming a part owner of your property.

Rental Property

If you rent your property there may be rules and regulations regarding running a business from the premises. If your rental agreement says you cannot run a business from the home then you cannot run any business at all from that premises.

If you want to start a business from a home you are renting, you may need to get the contract changed. You will need to consult whoever you deal with - your landlord or their agents. It may be that the landlord is using a standard contract and may not mind agreeing new terms, however if this is the case then make sure you get it in writing and double check, or take legal advice to make sure that what they say is okay, otherwise they could later use it against you as breach of contract.

Restrictive Covenants

Especially in older properties, you may find that the deeds contain clauses that prevent you from carrying out certain activities and running a food business may be one of them. You should consult your solicitor about this.

Environmental Health

You will need to speak to the Environmental Health Department (EHD) in the borough or district council in your area. The Environmental Health Officers (EHO) there will be able to give you advice on hygiene and safety especially relevant to your particular food business. They are in the best position to determine which parts of food law apply to you.

It is a legal requirement that you register your food business premises with your local authority. This must be done at least 28 days before you start running your business. You can be fined or even imprisoned for failing to register a food business.

Details on registering with your local environmental health service can be obtained by calling your local authority or visiting their website. Registration is a formality, it cannot be refused and is free. It applies to all commercial food businesses and if you have more than one premises, then every one must be registered. If you have a premises in another local authority area you must register with each authority separately.

You must also make sure that your local authority has up-to-date information about your premises, and tell them if you change significantly what you do in your business.

Your food business premises should be in a good state of repair, clean and free of pests. The rules require that you have clean drinking water, separate hand-wash facilities from food preparation (this may be in a nearby toilet if you use your home kitchen), good ventilation and lighting, good drainage, waste and rubbish facilities. You will need good wipe-clean surfaces and toilet facilities should also be available.

Using your own kitchen will mean you are working in a space which was not purpose-built for your business. You will need to be able to keep all pets out of the rooms you use. There should also be no soft furnishings in the rooms used for food production.

If you are having modifications made to accommodate your food business, contact your local EHO. They are able to advise on works before you start and, if requested, they can visit your premises for a consultation. EHO's can answer many of your questions. They are there to help and support you and their advice may be invaluable.

The EHO will appreciate that you are running a business from your home, they will expect to see children or pets and will guide and advise you on good working practice while you are operating your food business from your home.

Once you have completed registration, you are able to start trading.

It is your responsibility to maintain a registered business premises and comply with the law to produce food safely.

You are probably only storing and preparing low risk food, such as cakes, and therefore your local authority EHO will send you a questionnaire when you register. This questionnaire will help the EHO decide whether an inspection is necessary. If you are preparing higher risk foods such as buffets and hot meals, your local authority EHO will probably arrange an inspection shortly after you have registered.

Once you have registered your premises and obtained licences (if required), an Environmental Health Officer has the right to visit and they are not required to contact you first. In reality, as a business run from home, an EHO will not presume to turn up unannounced. You will normally be contacted to arrange a time if required. It's up to you to have any information they may require to hand – this will include details of business owner, directors (if appropriate), insurances, machinery maintenance records, supplier details and recorded evidence of good working practices.

Local authority EHO's can vary enormously in how they conduct their inspections. Some may require much more detail of your premises and the business you run than others. Some require higher levels of food labelling, evidence of temperature checks and so on, but they are there to help you attain the best standards to meet their approval.

You can be prosecuted and fined up to £5,000 if they feel you have obstructed them in any way.

Premises for Food Business

Full information on premises for a food business is available on the Food Standards Agency website:
http://www.food.gov.uk/business-industry/caterers/startingup/

The site carries a lot of useful information and guidance.

The following is a brief synopsis of the FSA's guidelines.

These points apply to all of the rooms or buildings that you will use in your food business:

- Keep your premises clean, well maintained and in a good state of repair.
- Provide adequate maintenance and cleaning.
- Avoid and minimise any possibility of airborne contamination.
- Prevent build-up of dirt and avoid contact with toxic materials.
- Prevent condensation, mould or any shedding of particles into food.
- Have enough space to carry out all your tasks hygienically.
- Ensure good food hygiene practices.
- Protect against contamination and maintain pest control.
- Make sure handling and storing food is carried out at appropriate temperatures.
- Make sure temperatures are monitored and, where necessary, recorded.

Choosing new premises or making changes to premises you already have:

It's a good idea to ask your local authority for advice relating to hand-washing and toilet facilities, particularly in relation to the home environment:

- You must have adequate toilet facilities which do not open directly into the food handling area.
- You must have hand-wash basins, suitably located and used only for hands with hot and cold running water, soap and suitable drying facilities.
- Where necessary, you should have a separate sink for washing food.

Concerning ventilation:

- You must have adequate ventilation, either natural or mechanical (e.g. extractor fans).
- Ventilation systems must be accessible for cleaning and maintenance.
- Toilets must have suitable ventilation.

Other general requirements:

- You must have adequate lighting, either natural and/or artificial.
- Drainage facilities must be adequate for the purpose, avoiding any risk of contamination.
- If you have staff, you must provide facilities for them to change their clothes, where necessary.
- You must not store cleaning products in areas where food is handled.

There are special requirements for rooms where you prepare, treat or process food:

- The design and layout must allow good food hygiene practices.
- Floor surfaces must be maintained and be easy to clean and disinfect where necessary.
- Floor surfaces need to be made of impervious materials that are washable and non-toxic.
- Walls should be impervious, in good condition and easy to clean.
- Ceilings and overhead fixtures must be finished to prevent build up of dirt.
- Windows, doors and other openings should be easy to clean and disinfect.
- Where necessary, insect-proof screens should be fitted to opening windows and doors.
- Where open windows would cause contamination, they must be closed while producing food.
- Surfaces must be maintained in a sound condition and be easy to clean and disinfect.
- You must have an adequate supply of hot and cold water
- You must have adequate cleaning, disinfecting and storing utensils and equipment.
- Where necessary, you must have food washing facilities. The water must be of drinking quality and the facilities must be kept clean and, where necessary, disinfected.

Licences

You will only be required to hold licences if you:
- Supply and/or sell alcohol.
- Sell hot foods and drinks between 11pm and 5am.
- Provide entertainment, such as cinema, theatre, and some live music.
- Sell food from a van or stand on the street.

Contact your authority if you require information on applying for these licences.

Displaying your licence

Individual councils will have their own rules on how licences should be displayed. It is usual that your approved status is shown on the food products themselves.

Fines and penalties

It's a criminal offence to run unapproved food premises and not to hold relevant licences. You can be prosecuted for doing so.

Chapter 5

Running a Food Business

Rules and Regulations

This chapter deals with the law and environmental health regulations. Much of the content of this chapter is expanded upon in the following chapter, dealing directly with food safety.

Even if you are planning to run your business from home, food hygiene and preparation rules apply to any premises in which food is prepared. Anyone who handles food, or whose actions could affect its safety, must follow the regulations. This includes people who sell food, whether to retailers or to the public, and anyone who cleans items which come into contact with food.

The main regulations you will have to be aware of are: Regulation (EC) No. 852/2004 on the hygiene of foodstuffs, and The Food Hygiene Regulations 2006.

Although Food Hygiene Regulations 2006 applies specifically to England, there are equivalents for Scotland, Wales and Northern Ireland.

The regulations set out the basic hygiene requirements for all aspects of your business, from your premises and facilities to the personal hygiene of your staff. A key requirement of the law is that you are able to show what you do to process food safely and that you have written records to show this.

Many of the regulations will not appear relevant to you, or are clearly directed at the larger food business, but the principles are all the same. Reading <u>all</u> the guidelines will ensure you do not miss anything pertinent to your particular setup.

Food Standards Agency (FSA)

The Food Standards Agency is responsible for food safety and food hygiene across the UK. Their job is protecting the public, regulating the food industry and enforcing food standards. They work with businesses to help them produce safe food. The FSA also work with local authorities to enforce food safety regulations. Research related to food safety issues is commissioned by the FSA.

The FSA say "Everything we do reflects our vision of 'Safer food for the nation'. We aim to ensure that food produced or sold in the UK is safe to eat, consumers have the information they need to make informed choices about where and what they eat and that regulation and enforcement is risk-based and focused on improving public health."

You can keep yourself informed about up-to-date news on the FSA website at www.food.gov.uk/news-updates. It contains news of any current food hygiene issues and information about latest campaigns, consultations, food recalls and allergy alerts.

The FSA have a lot of helpful information for those thinking of, or starting their own food business. They have detailed information in their guides available on their website:
- Starting Up – Your first steps to running a catering business (PDF format).
- Food Hygiene – A Guide For Businesses (PDF format).
- Safer Food Better Business.
You can order these guides in hard copy by calling 0845 606 0667.

The booklets (or online guides) focus on the main areas you need to consider when running a food business and point you in the right direction for further assistance if required.

The Trading Standards Department of your local county council has responsibility for food law enforcement. This includes the checking of product labels. If you need any advice on the labelling of specific food products, it is a good idea to contact them. There is further information on labelling on the FSA's website but if you have greater need of labelling guidelines, there are consultants who specifically deal with this sort of thing.

Training

It is not law that you should hold a food hygiene certificate – it is not mandatory for anyone, full-time or at one-off events. If you are working with food you do need to be instructed, trained and supervised as necessary in food hygiene processes appropriate to the work you carry out.

It is strongly recommended that you study for a food hygiene qualification as this provides written evidence of your due diligence to providing food safely.

Local colleges, or your local authority will have information on courses in food hygiene, but they can also be accessed online. Food hygiene courses are designed to equip you with skills and knowledge to prepare and handle food hygienically.

The Food Hygiene level 2 (CIEH) course is a recognised minimum requirement for anyone handling food. It is approved by the Chartered Institute of Environmental Health and meets the requirements of the Food Safety Act 1990 and the Food Safety Regulations 1995.

HACCP

Much of the information included here is also available on the FSA website at: http://www.food.gov.uk/business-industry/caterers/haccp

74

HACCP (Hazard Analysis and Critical Control Point) is a system that your local Environmental Health Officer (EHO) will check as part of their routine when inspecting a premises.

It is a system that helps food businesses look at how they handle food and introduces procedures to make sure the food produced is safe to eat.

The EHO will need to see evidence that a HACCP-based food safety management system in place.

What is HACCP?

HACCP (Hazard Analysis and Critical Control Point) is a way of managing food safety and is based on procedures, put in place to control hazards.

HACCPs involves:
- Looking at what you do in your business and looking for what could go wrong.
- Identifying the 'critical control points' – the places you need to focus effort to prevent or reduce hazards to a safe level.
- Putting in place procedures to make sure hazards are controlled at your critical control points.
- Deciding what action you need to take if something goes wrong.
- Making sure that your procedures are working.
- Keep appropriate records to show your procedures are working.

HACCP may seem to be very complicated, but it doesn't have to be. The important thing is to have food safety management procedures that are appropriate for your business. There are packs produced by the Food Standards Agency (FSA) that can help you put these procedures in place.

HACCP guidance

For small food businesses, 'Safer Food, Better Business' (SFBB) helps you put in place food safety management procedures based on HACCP and which will ensure you comply with food hygiene regulations.

75

The SFBB pack details these guidelines:
- You must put in place 'food safety management procedures' based on the principles of HACCP.
- You must also keep up-to-date documents and records relating to your procedures.
- Review your procedures if you change what you produce or how you work.

This means that you must have procedures in place to manage food safety 'hazards' in your business. You must write these procedures down and update them as necessary. Make sure you keep records that can be checked by your local authority.

The regulations are designed to be flexible, so the procedures may be made relative to the size of your business and the type of work you do. This means that many small businesses will have quite simple procedures and records.

If you handle both raw and ready-to-eat food you may need to consider extra procedures for the control of harmful bacteria.

What is a hazard?

A hazard is something that could be dangerous. And there are lots of different hazards. When we are talking about hazards in relation to food, a hazard is something that could mean that food will not be safe to eat.

Food safety hazards can be:
- Microbiological – involving harmful bacteria, e.g. when certain food is kept out of the fridge for too long and bacteria grow in it.
- Chemical – involving chemicals getting into food, e.g. cleaning products or pest control chemicals.
- Physical – involving objects getting into food, e.g. broken glass or pieces of packaging.

Hazards can happen at any stage in your business – from taking deliveries to serving customers.

Food safety management procedures.

You can develop your own procedures based on the principles of HACCP. Alternatively you can use a pack produced by the FSA or your local authority, or a food industry guide recognised by the FSA, to help you comply with the law.

These procedures may not be necessary for some businesses with very simple processes. In this case, businesses can comply with the legal requirement by following good hygiene practice. Contact your local authority for advice on whether this applies to you. Some regulations will still need to be complied with.

Safer Food, Better Business

Safer Food, Better Business (SFBB) is an innovative and practical approach to food safety management used in England and Wales. It helps small businesses with food safety management procedures and food hygiene regulations.

It is there to help you to:
● Comply with food hygiene regulations.
● Show what you do to make food safely.
● Train staff.
● Protect your business's reputation.
● Improve your business, such as by wasting less food.

The SFBB guides are available for many different areas of the food industry:
● SFBB for caterers (this is us!) to help small catering businesses comply with food hygiene regulations.
● SFBB for retailers to help retail businesses across the UK comply with food hygiene regulations.
● SFBB for different cuisines for small Chinese, Indian, Pakistani, Bangladeshi and Sri Lankan cuisines.
● SFBB in other languages for Chinese cuisine is available in Traditional Chinese.
● SFBB for childminders including information on feeding babies and children.

- SFBB for residential care homes is a supplement to their stringent food safety procedures
- SFBB teaching resources for colleges intended to promote understanding of SFBB among catering students.

The guide relevant to your business can be viewed online on the FSA website or you can download the full guide containing all the information required. It contains an introduction explaining how to use the pack. It allows you to electronically complete the sections, prior to printing. This provides a record of all your processes for dealing with cross-contamination, cleaning, chilling, cooking, management and a diary to record daily checks and procedures and detail any changes, developments or problems.

You can print out the diary refill separately if you only need that part of the pack or if you prefer, you can download the diary pages, fill them in, name them with the appropriate month and year and store them electronically.

You should store all your completed diary pages safely until your next visit from a local authority enforcement officer. During the visit he or she may want to look at and/or retain your diary pages. Check with the enforcement officer how long he or she wants you to keep them.

There is also a DVD guide to help with staff training and is available in 16 different languages. You can download a copy to your computer or you can view it online at: www.food.gov.uk/sfbbtraining

Food safety management packs have different names for different countries
- **England and Wales**
  'Safer Food, Better Business' as described above.
- **Scotland**
  The FSA in Scotland has drawn on expertise from the food industry including small businesses, local authorities and the Scottish Food Advisory Committee to develop a HACCP-based system called 'CookSafe'. This is available in English, Chinese, Bengali, Urdu and Punjabi. 'RetailSafe' is also available for retailers. Visit www.food.gov.uk to find out more.
- **Northern Ireland**
  The FSA in Northern Ireland has produced guidance for the

catering sector called 'Safe Catering', by working with caterers and local authorities. This guidance, which has been developed and refined over a number of years, is widely accepted by the catering sector in Northern Ireland. Businesses should contact their local authority for information.

Food businesses do not have to use any particular pack or model, but they must make sure they have food safety management procedures that are suitable for their business. Some businesses will already have a suitable system, which they can continue to use.

Note: The FSA also produce a clear basic fact sheet 'Working with Food?' which can be displayed in any food preparation environment. It provides an on-site reminder of what anyone in your establishment needs to know or do before you start working with food.

Transport

Vehicles and/or containers used to transport food must be kept clean and maintained and in good repair and condition, to protect food from contamination. Where necessary, they must be designed and constructed to allow adequate cleaning and/or disinfection.

Items used to hold food (e.g. boxes) in vehicles and/or containers must not be used for transporting anything other than food where this may cause contamination.

Where vehicles and/or containers are used for transporting anything other than food, or for transporting different types of food at the same time, you must separate products effectively, where necessary.

Where vehicles and/or containers have been used for transporting anything other than food or for transporting different foods, you must clean effectively between loads to avoid the risk of contamination.

Food in vehicles and/or containers must be placed and protected in a way that minimises the risk of contamination.

Where necessary, vehicles and/or containers used for transporting food must be capable of keeping food at appropriate temperatures and allow those temperatures to be monitored.

Equipment

All items, fittings and equipment that food touches must be:
- Cleaned effectively to avoid any risk of contamination.
- Made of appropriate materials and kept in good order to enable effective cleaning except for non-returnable containers and packaging.
- Installed in a way that allows adequate cleaning of the equipment and the surrounding area.
- Fitted, where necessary, with an appropriate temperature sensor.
- If chemicals are used on equipment and containers, they must be used in accordance with good practice.

Food Waste and Rubbish

Organise your food waste, rubbish and recycling collection:-
- You must remove food waste and other rubbish from rooms where food is present as quickly as possible.
- You must put food waste and other rubbish in containers that can be closed. These containers must be of appropriate construction, kept in sound condition, be easy to clean and disinfect.
- You must have adequate facilities for storing and disposing of food waste and other rubbish. These must be kept clean and, where necessary, free of animals and pests.
- You must get rid of all waste in a hygienic and environmentally friendly way, in accordance with legislation.
- The waste must not be a direct or indirect source of

contamination. For example it must not attract pests, or touch surfaces that food is prepared on.

Water Supply

Your water supply must meet certain standards:
- You must have an adequate supply of drinking water.
- Where non-potable water (i.e. not of drinking quality) is used in your business, (e.g., for fire control, steam production, refrigeration, etc.) it must not connect with, or be able to get into, the systems for drinking water.
- If recycled water is used, it must not present a risk of contamination. It must be of the same standard as potable (drinking quality) water, unless you can satisfy your local authority otherwise.
- Ice that is touched by food, or may contaminate food (including drinks), must be made from drinking water. Ice must be made, handled and stored in ways that protect it from contamination.
- Steam that is used directly in contact with food must not contain anything likely to contaminate the food.
- If you heat food in hermetically sealed containers, you must make sure that the water you use to cool the containers is not a source of contamination for the food.

Family, Pets and Plants!

Your family and kitchen use

Separating family and business use of the kitchen can be awkward but it is essential for good food hygiene. When preparing food as part of your business you must not prepare food for your family. You must limit access to the kitchen by children, and other people during food preparation for business purposes. Normal routine activities such as washing clothes must not be carried out at such times.

Your pets and your kitchen

Pets must be excluded from the kitchen during food preparation and pet food should be kept well away from all food production and storage areas.

Plants and other decorative items

Make sure that any plants and decorative items that you might normally have in your kitchen are out of the way when you are processing food for business purposes. This will prevent contamination from anything falling into the food.

Inspections

Local authorities are responsible for enforcing food hygiene laws. If you run a business that makes or prepares food, it will be inspected to make sure you are following food law.

The inspectors will be enforcement officers from your local authority (or district council in Northern Ireland). These officers might come on a routine inspection, or they might visit because of a complaint.

They have the right to enter and inspect your premises at any reasonable time and usually come without telling you first. The exception is the home-based food business where an inspection will usually have to be arranged.

What inspectors do

Inspectors must follow the Food Standards Agency's Framework Agreement on local authority food law enforcement, and the Food Law Code of Practice when making visits. The Framework Agreement, can be found on the FSA website. The framework sets standards for how local authorities carry out their enforcement duties.

Inspectors should show you identification when they arrive and be polite throughout the visit. They should always give you feedback on an inspection. They will tell you about any problems they have identified and advise you about how these problems can be avoided.

If inspectors advise you to do something, they must tell you whether you need to do it to comply with the law, or whether it is good practice. You must be given, in writing, the details of reasons for any action you are asked to take, as a result of the inspection. The inspectors must state the details of the law if they decide that you are breaking a law.

You should be given a reasonable amount of time to make changes, except where there is an immediate risk to public health. The inspector must also tell you how you can appeal against their actions.

Action an inspector can take
When they think it is necessary, officers can take 'enforcement action' to protect the public.
This can include:
- Taking samples and photographs of food.
- Inspecting your records.
- Writing you a letter asking you to put right any problems.
- Seizing suspect foods.
- Serving a formal, legal notice that sets out certain things you must do, or forbidding you from using certain processes, premises or equipment.
- Recommending prosecution in serious cases.

If they serve you with a notice, it will be one of three main types:
1. **'Hygiene improvement notice'** or **'food labelling improvement notice'** – sets out certain things that you must do to comply, if your business is breaking the law.
2. **'Hygiene emergency prohibition notice'** – forbids the use of certain processes, premises or equipment and must be confirmed by a court.
3. **'Remedial action notice'** – forbids the use of certain processes, premises or equipment, or imposes conditions on how a process is carried out. It's similar to a hygiene emergency prohibition

notice, but it does not need to be confirmed by a court. (This type of notice applies to approved establishments only in England, Wales and Northern Ireland, and can be used for any food establishment in Scotland).

It is a criminal offence not to comply with a notice once served. Inspectors can also recommend a prosecution, in serious cases. If a prosecution is successful, the court may forbid you from using certain processes, premises or equipment, or you could be banned from managing a food business. It could also lead to a fine or imprisonment.

For more information, see the 'Food law inspections and your business' booklet at:
www.food.gov.uk/food-law-inspections

Food law inspections and your business

Inspections are there to make sure food produced is safe to eat. To do this, they will look at:
- Your premises.
- The kinds of food you make or prepare (how you work).
- Your food safety management system.

Where labelling is appropriate make sure descriptions are clear and not misleading. The inspectors will look at how you describe food, for example on a label, to make sure the description is not misleading for customers - labelling is covered in more detail later.

We have already covered information about the legal requirements on food safety and hygiene. You can also contact the Environmental Health service at your local authority for advice regarding inspections.

Frequency of inspections

How often the inspectors routinely inspect your business depends on the type of business and its previous record. Some premises might be inspected at least every six months, others much less often. It is perfectly usual for a small home cake making business not to see an inspector for years after the initial setup of the business. Reports indicate that it is not considered a high risk business.

Making an appeal

All local authorities must have a formal procedure to deal with complaints about its service. You should contact the head of Environmental Health or Trading Standards services at your local authority, if you do not agree with action taken by an inspector. This will help you see if the problem can be resolved through talking or writing letters. If you still disagree after that, you could approach your local councillor.

You can contact your local government or public services ombudsman if you are not happy with a local authority's complaints process:
- England Local Government Ombudsman.
- Scotland Public Services Ombudsman.
- Wales Public Services Ombudsman.
- Northern Ireland Ombudsman.
Contact details for these can be found at the back of this book.

You can appeal to the magistrates' court (or a Sheriff in Scotland) about a local authority's decision to issue a hygiene improvement notice or remedial notice, or not to lift a hygiene emergency prohibition order.

When there is a ban on an individual, this can only be lifted by the court. You can attend the court hearing if you want to. If the court decides that premises have been shut without proper reason, or food has been wrongly seized or detained, you have a right to compensation.

Further information

The FSA and your local authority EHO can advise you about food law and the food safety for your specific business.

Food Hygiene Rating Systems

The Food Hygiene Rating System (FHRS) now has in place a system which can rate home businesses. The take up of the system may vary between borough councils. Until recently many councils would not rate home businesses due to the inability to drop in unannounced. But now, with a report of confidence in the management and a visit, a home based food business can qualify for the FHRS.

Food Hygiene Rating Scheme for customers

The FHRS helps customers choose where to eat out or shop for food by giving you information about the hygiene standards of food businesses including restaurants, pubs, cafés, takeaways, bakeries, hotels and other places including supermarkets and food shops. Ratings are also given to other places where you may eat away from home, such as schools, hospitals and residential care homes.

Hygiene standards of a food business are not apparent on appearance alone. The FHRS gives you an idea of what is going on in a businesses kitchen, or behind closed doors. The scheme also encourages businesses to improve hygiene standards.

The scheme is run by local authorities in England, Wales and Northern Ireland in partnership with the Food Standards Agency. Local authorities are responsible for carrying out inspections of food businesses to check that they meet the requirements of food hygiene law. They give businesses food hygiene ratings based on their of inspections and the information is published on the Food Standards Agency's website: food.gov.uk/ratings.

The FHRS is a national scheme run in England, Wales and Northern Ireland with a similar scheme is running in Scotland. The scheme was set up and, in the most part, running to it's full extent in 99% of local authority areas by summer 2013.

A similar scheme called the 'Food Hygiene Information Scheme' is run in Scotland. You can access inspection results of businesses in Scotland and read more about the scheme run in Scotland. Details can be accessed via www.foodstandards.gov.scot

Some places where you might buy and/or consume food are not given a rating. This is because they are a low risk businesses, for example, a newsagent selling only wrapped sweets. These businesses might be listed on this website, but will be shown to be 'exempt' from the scheme.

Food Hygiene Rating Scheme for food businesses

If you serve or supply food direct to the public, you can be covered by the FHRS. This means that when your business is inspected, you will be given a hygiene rating. At the bottom of the scale is '0' meaning urgent improvement is required. At the top of the scale is '5' meaning that the hygiene standards are very good. If the top rating is not given, the officer will explain to you what improvements are needed and what action taken so you can improve your hygiene rating.

In Scotland, you will be given a 'Pass' or 'Improvement Required' result as part of the Food Hygiene Information Scheme.

You will be given a certificate with your rating or result. Display this to show your customers how good your hygiene standards are. Customers will also be able to look up the ratings of businesses on the Food Standards Agency's website at food.gov.uk/ratings

How to get your rating

A food safety officer from the local authority where the business is located, will inspect the business to check that it meets the requirements of food hygiene law. For home businesses, if you have not been contacted for an inspection, you can contact the local authority to action one. No inspection, no rating.

At the inspection, the officer will:
- Check how hygienically the food is handled, how it is prepared, cooked, re-heated, cooled and stored.
- Check the condition of the structure of the buildings, cleanliness,

layout, lighting, ventilation and other facilities.

- Look at how the business manages what it does to make sure food is safe. The officer needs to see evidence to give him or her confidence that standards will continue to be maintained in the future.

Each of these elements is essential to ensure food hygiene standards meet requirements, and the food served or sold, is safe to eat.

You can achieve the necessary levels of food safety by demonstrating that you maintain high hygienic standards in all areas of food preparation:

- The personal hygiene of staff e.g. clean over-clothing (such as aprons), appropriate head-wear, minimal jewellery and regular and appropriate hand washing.
- Control measures in place to prevent cross contamination e.g. use of separate areas for handling raw and cooked foods, proper use of colour coded chopping boards, and correct use of appropriate cleaning chemicals.
- Foods are stored at the correct temperature e.g. food stored in fridges is maintained at less than 8°C and that the chill chain is protected.
- Foods are properly cooked, re-heated and cooled e.g. foods are cooked to 75°C or hotter and are checked visually for signs of thorough cooking, and foods are cooled quickly and, as necessary refrigerated.

The condition and structure of the premises should be, for example:

- A suitable structure which is clean and in good repair throughout.
- Adequate natural/artificial lighting.
- Adequate natural/artificial ventilation.
- A structure proofed against pest entry.

How the business manages and records what it does to make sure food is safe is a legal requirement for food businesses. This should:

- Identify and show an understanding of the food safety hazards (microbiological, physical and chemical) within the business.
- Provide evidence that measures have been taken to effectively control these hazards and that these measures are reviewed as appropriate.

- Provide evidence that all food handlers are supervised and instructed and/or trained in food hygiene matters in order that they produce food that is safe to eat.

All the above processes are identified in The Food Standards Agency's food safety management system - Safer Food, Better Business.

Achieving the top rating

To get the best possible rating, you should look at your last food hygiene inspection report to check that you've taken all of the actions needed to ensure that you meet legal requirements - if you can't find your last report, contact your local authority or the FSA and they will be able to supply you with a copy.

At your next inspection, the food safety officer will be able to give you advice if necessary to help you achieve and maintain the best rating possible.

Elements of the FHRS

The food hygiene rating reflects the hygiene standards found by the Food Safety Officer at the time of the inspection. These officers are specially trained to assess food hygiene standards.

The rating given will show how well the business is doing overall. It will also take note of things most in need of improving and assess the level of risk to people's health. Each of these three elements is checked to make sure that food hygiene standards meet requirements and the food served or sold is safe to eat.

Some businesses will do well in some areas and less well in others, but good practise needs to be demonstrated in all three areas to achieve required standards to gain the highest rating '5'.

Businesses rating '0' are probably performing poorly in all three elements and are likely to have a history of serious problems. They will not be able to demonstrate sufficient good food practise to make sure the food is safe.

Frequency of inspections for the FHRS

Each time the business is inspected by a food safety officer, a new rating can be given.

How often inspections take place depends on the potential risk to people's health if something goes wrong. This depends on the type of food being handled and the processes that are carried out before the food is sold or served to the public.

Higher risk businesses, e.g. those preparing raw meat, are inspected more often than, for example, a small home baker who poses a much lower risk. The time between inspections varies from six months for the highest risk business to two years for lower risk businesses. For some very low risk businesses, the interval between inspections may be even greater.

In some cases, a business may ask its local authority for a visit to be carried out before the next planned inspection is due. For example, if the business was given a rating below the top one of '5' and has made improvements to hygiene standards. The Food Safety Officer can check the improvements made and see if a new rating should be given.

Local authorities plan a programme of inspections every year so that the Food Safety Officers can focus on those businesses that have poorer hygiene standards. This can dictate the overall frequency of inspections.

If the local authority receives a complaint or information about a business which suggests hygiene standards are not being maintained, the local authority will investigate even if they are not due to inspect. They may re-evaluate the business and review their hygiene rating.

Even if a rating was given a long time ago, the rating remains. Each rating is based on the most recent inspection and you may wish to consider inviting an inspection if you have done work to improve your rating.

Some types of food business present a low risk to people's health.

In such cases, the most recent inspection may have been some time ago. The local authority can monitor the business to check it is maintaining hygiene standards in other ways. For example, by a short visit to the premises to check things, or by getting the business to complete a questionnaire. If these checks reveal anything that might indicate that hygiene standards have deteriorated, the officer will carry out an inspection and the business will get a new rating.

All businesses should be able to achieve the top rating. If you do not, the Food Safety Officer will tell you what improvements need to be made to achieve a higher rating. They can give you practical advice on how to make the improvements. You will be pointed towards the FSA and tools, such as 'Safer Food, Better Business', which can help you manage and improve food hygiene.

Businesses with poor ratings are not always closed. If you receive a '0' or '1' rating, you must make urgent or major improvements to hygiene standards. The local authority Food Safety Officer will use a number of enforcement tools as well as giving advice and guidance to make sure these improvements are made. You will also be told how quickly these improvements must be made and this will depend on the type of issue that needs to be addressed.

If an officer finds hygiene standards are very poor and there is an imminent risk to health, he or she must take action to make sure that consumers are protected. This could mean prohibiting part of an operation or closing the business down completely.

As a business you will receive a ratings sticker and certificate which you can display in a place where your customers will easily see them. The stickers and certificates also show the date the hygiene standards were assessed by the local authority. You do not have to display your rating but why hide a '5' rating?

Consider also, that if you do not show your rating, even if it is not a '5', your customers may be left wondering just how safe your food practices are. Putting your hygiene rating on show is a good advertisement for your business, demonstrating that your business meets the requirements of food hygiene law. In Wales it is compulsory for food businesses to display their hygiene rating sticker.

Some local authorities are only gradually rolling out the scheme which means that you may not receive a rating until your business is next inspected, which may be a while if you are in the low risk group. You might want to consider asking your authority if it is possible to bring an inspection forward so that you can receive a rating.

Your right to appeal and right to reply

If you think the rating given is unfair or wrong, you should talk to the local authority Food Safety Officer that inspected the business about why the rating was given. If you still think that the rating is unfair or wrong, you can appeal in writing. To appeal, you can download an appeal form from the FSA or your local authority. Send it to your local authority's lead Environmental Health Officer within 14 days (this includes weekends and public holidays) of being told what your rating is.

As an owner or manager of a food business you also have a 'right to reply'; this is different from an appeal. You can download a right to reply form and send it to your local authority to tell the Food Safety Officer how your business has improved hygiene practises, or to say if there were unusual circumstances at the time of an inspection. Your 'right to reply' will be published online by the local authority with the business' hygiene rating.

Re-visits for a new rating

You can ask the local authority to re-visit to get a new rating, but only if the improvements to hygiene that the local authority Food Safety Officer told the business about at the last inspection have been made. You can only ask the local authority for a re-visit to be carried out once before the date of the next planned inspection. Any food business can download a re-visit form and send it to their local authority.

Advertising your rating

Food businesses can advertise their hygiene ratings on their menus or websites. It is good for your businesses to show your customers how seriously you take food hygiene. Your local authority food safety officer can provide you with the official artwork that you can use.

You should only display or advertise your current rating otherwise you will mislead customers and may be committing an offence under trading standards legislation.

You can contact the Food Hygiene Ratings Team via email to: hygiene ratings@foodstandards.gsi.gov.uk or by calling: 020 7276 8445. You can also write to: Food Hygiene Ratings Team, Aviation House, 125 Kingsway, London WC2B 6HN

Health and Safety

Risk assessments and health and safety

Health and safety is important for employers and those who want to make sure their business complies with health and safety law. In general, the laws apply to all businesses, no matter how small provided you employ staff. As an employer, or a self-employed person, you are responsible for health and safety in your business. You must take precautions to reduce risks and provide a safe working environment.

You are required to protect people as far as 'reasonably practicable' though it is not presumed that you can totally eliminate all risks. A risk assessment is an important step in protecting your workers (if you have any) and your business, as well as complying with the law. In many instances straightforward measures can readily control risks. For most businesses that means simple, cheap and effective measures to ensure your most valuable asset – your workforce – is protected.

A risk assessment is simply a careful examination of what, in your work, could cause harm to people, so that you can weigh up whether you have taken enough precautions or should do more to prevent harm.

Workers and others have a right to be protected from harm caused by a failure to take reasonable control measures. Accidents and ill health can ruin lives and affect your business too. As an employer, you are legally required to assess the risks in your workplace so that you put in place a plan to control the risks.

In particular, if you rent or use business premises separate from your home and/or you employ people, you must carry out a Health and Safety Risk Assessment in the workplace and take action to remove any hazards.

You'll normally be responsible for:
- Fire safety.
- Safety of electrical equipment.
- Gas safety - maintaining equipment according to the manufacturer's instructions, including annual inspections.
- Managing asbestos.

You're also responsible for providing:
- A reasonable temperature.
- Enough space, ventilation and lighting.
- Toilets and washing facilities.
- Drinking water.
- Safety and first aid equipment.

The Health and Safety Executive's 'Workplace Health, Safety and Welfare: a Short Guide' has more details including their guidelines which show how you can assess the risks in your workplace.

Step 1 - Identify the hazards.
Step 2 - Decide who might be harmed and how.
Step 3 - Evaluate the risks and decide on precautions.
Step 4 - Record your findings and implement them.
Step 5 - Review your assessment and update if necessary.

If you don't follow health and safety rules you can be prosecuted. The main law covering health and safety at work in the UK is the Health and Safety at Work Act 1974. The Health and Safety Executive (HSE) and local councils are responsible for making sure you follow the law. You can access more information of the Health and Safety Executive's website: www.hse.gov.uk

Food Assurance Schemes

These are voluntary food assurance schemes such as Red Tractor or Lion Eggs. These schemes let customers know food has been produced to certain standards e.g. on food safety or animal welfare.

There is none which fit the home cake decorators business but using products that are part of these assurance schemes will show due diligence.

British Lion Code of Practice

British Lion eggs account for more than 85% of UK egg production. The Lion mark denotes eggs that have been subjected to controls including vaccinations, registration and 'passport' systems for traceability, hygiene controls including Salmonella testing, stringent feed controls, eggs stamped on farm with the farm code and production method and best-before date and Lion logo printed on the shell of Lion Quality eggs as well as on the egg box.

The Lion Quality mark, which is a registered trademark, can only be used by subscribers to the British Egg Industry Council on eggs which have been produced in accordance with UK and EU law and the Lion Quality Code of Practice.

Buy eggs from a reputable retailer where they will have been transported and stored at the correct temperature (below 20°C). Keep eggs refrigerated after purchase, in their box and, as eggs are porous, away from strong-smelling foods. Make sure you use eggs by the 'best before' date shown on the egg or box - for Lion Quality eggs, this guarantees that they are fresher than required by law.

Organic certification

If you produce or prepare organic food, you must be certified by one of the organic control bodies if you want to sell or label it as such. Organic food production within the EU is strictly regulated.

If you are a provider of organic food, or if you market organic products, you must be registered with an approved organic control body (CB). You must also be inspected at least once a year to ensure that you meet the EU-wide standards. Only then can your products legally be labelled and marketed as 'organic'.

Chapter 6

Food Safety for Businesses

Please Note: Even though there might not be a specific legal requirement behind food safety guidelines, it is very important to follow the advice in this section as legal action may be taken if you do not follow the guidelines and this results in food poisoning or illness.

Advice regarding food safety is available on the Food Standards Agency's website: http://www.food.gov.uk

General Guidelines

It is essential that you practise good food hygiene to make and sell food that is safe to eat. It is vital that you and your staff understand good food hygiene. Food businesses are required by law, to ensure that food handlers are supervised, instructed and/or trained in food hygiene relevant to their work to enable them to handle food safely. Anyone providing the business's food safety management procedures must have received adequate training to enable them to do this.

In the UK, food handlers do not have to hold a food hygiene certificate although many food businesses will prefer they do.

Learning may be obtained through on-the-job training, self-study, publicly run courses or previous experience. UK food hygiene certificates do not usually have an expiry date. It is left to the discretion of the food business or Environmental Health Officer to decide whether a refresher course is needed, but a refresher of this qualification is usually recommended at least every three years. This will demonstrate 'due diligence' with regard to food safety.

CIEH Level 2 Awards in Food Safety has been developed to cover several areas of food business, addressing the growing need to make learning more relevant to specific business environments and meet the National Occupational Standards. The 'CIEH Level 2 Awards in Food Safety in Catering' provides the necessary training for the home-based cake decorating business.

Everyone who works with food has a special responsibility for safeguarding the health of consumers and ensure that the food they serve or sell is perfectly safe to eat. Food safety involves protecting food from anything that could cause harm and it protects everyone.

If you are working in the food industry, you need a firm grasp of the importance of food safety and knowledge of the systems, techniques and procedures involved. You need to understand how to control food safety risks (personal hygiene, food storage, cooking and handling) and have confidence and the necessary expertise to safely deliver quality food to customers.

Poor standards of food safety threaten people's health as well as your reputation, profits and jobs. It is against the law to serve or sell food that could harm health and the law says that people who work with food must protect food from contamination.

Food safety is largely a matter of common sense. The main points to remember when operating a safe food business can be reduced to "the four C's":
- Cross-contamination.
- Cleaning.
- Chilling.
- Cooking.

Cross-contamination
Cross-contamination is when bacteria are spread between food,

surfaces or equipment. It is most likely to happen when raw food touches (or drips onto) ready-to-eat food, equipment or surfaces. Cross-contamination is one of the most common causes of food poisoning.

Cleaning
Effective cleaning gets rid of bacteria on hands, equipment and surfaces. So it helps to stop harmful bacteria from spreading onto food.

Chilling
Chilling food properly helps to stop harmful bacteria from growing. Some food needs to be kept chilled to keep it safe, for example food with a 'use by' date, cooked dishes and other ready-to-eat food such as prepared salads and desserts. It is very important not to leave these types of food standing around at room temperature.

Cooking
Thorough cooking kills most harmful bacteria in food. So it is extremely important to make sure that food is cooked properly.

Understanding how these processes affect the food you prepare and how they can be used or/and controlled safely, for the protection of food, will allow you to maintain a safe food environment.

In the following sections you will read how the four C's are relevant in many different areas of the food business and we give details on how an environment for the safe production of food can be maintained.

Hazards to Food

Hazards are anything that could cause harm to consumers. This could be illness, physical harm or discomfort. Hazards are either biological (micro-organisms), physical or chemical. There are many possible hazards to food that may present at many different stages of the food process.

As a food handler, you need to help stop possible hazards from causing actual harm. You are required to reduce direct threat by taking measures to prevent contamination.

Contaminants

Examples of biological hazards might include:
- Bacteria.
- Viruses.
- Fungi, such as moulds and yeasts.
- Microscopic parasites.

Examples of chemical hazards might include:
- Cleaning chemicals.
- Agricultural products, pesticides, fertilizers etc.
- Industrial products, cleaning agents etc.
- Pest bait in food premises.
- Dissolved metal from use of inappropriate metal containers.

Examples of physical hazards might include:
- Packaging materials, string, tape etc.
- Shell or bone fragments.
- Broken glass.
- Dust and dirt.
- Hair, fingernails.
- Jewellery.
- The bodies of insects and pests.

Even the simplest foods go through several food processing stages. Growing, harvesting, slaughtering, catching, processing, packing, transporting, storing, preparing, cooking, displaying, serving and selling are many of the stages that food will travel through.

There are hazards at all these stages. Hazards exist in the natural world and are also created by us. A hazard is a 'possible danger'. The aim is to prevent the hazard becoming an 'actual danger'.

Contamination happens as a result of an unrecognised hazard. It is the presence of something in food or drink that is objectionable or may be harmful. It starts the series of events that lead to food poisoning and

This is why food businesses must watch out for hazards to food.

Allergens

There are foods that are hazardous to a small number of individuals. These foods are described as allergens. These include foods like peanuts and seeds, that are perfectly safe for most people, but may cause illness to people who are unable to tolerate that food. Reactions may be mild but severe reactions may cause death if medical treatment is not given immediately.

A food allergy is an intolerance to that food that makes the immune system react as if the body is under attack. The reaction may occur only minutes after eating only a very small amount of a food or ingredient.

There is are wide range of symptoms, ranging from sickness, abdominal cramps, rash, diarrhoea, tingling or swelling of the mouth and throat and difficulties with speech or breathing. Anaphylactic shock is a reaction that can be life-threatening including a dramatic loss of blood pressure and unconsciousness.

Most individuals who have a food allergy are aware of it and know what they need to avoid. Many may still need help in identifying potential risk ingredients in food. They need to be able to trust the information provided by the food producer. Accuracy for labelling is essential where it is required.

You must also be careful not to transfer allergens to other foods. Special steps may be required including hand washing after handling allergens and keeping ingredients and utensils in segregated areas for dealing with food intended to be allergen free.

The most commonly found allergens include:
- Nuts, seeds and products made using these products.
- Shellfish and fish.
- Chocolate.
- Fruit.
- Milk and dairy products.
- Flour (gluten or/and wheat products).
- Food additives, colourants and flavour enhancers.

101

Physical hazards

Biological hazards are the most common cause of illness linked with food, but no one wants a fly in their soup and physical contamination can cause considerable upset, dissatisfaction and complaint. This is probably because the contaminant is visible, unlike most chemical or biological contaminants.

Glass, fingernails and bones are all physical contaminants that can be a choking hazard or be the cause of infections or bleeding. Even if a consumer is not injured by the contaminant they may be significantly upset by it.

There are, of course, natural physical hazards that are a natural part of the food, like leaves, shell, scales or bone. These are likely to be in many food premises.

It is up to consumers to watch out for contaminants in products which are sold 'whole' or with a warning that the product may contain bones.

For other products, the consumer expects that the food producer has done everything within their power to ensure the removal of physical contaminants, and this is backed up by the law.

Fruit and vegetables that may contain dirt, can easily contaminate other foods and should be well washed away from other foods that may be ready for packaging or consumption.

Individuals should take precautions to avoid being the cause of contamination. Hair, fingernails, jewellery, pens, buttons and plasters should all be kept neat, secure or removed whilst in food preparation areas. Wear protective clothing, tie hair back and remove jewellery.

Food packaging and poorly maintained buildings and equipment can also be the source of physical contamination. Ineffective cleaning and rubbish disposal can also be causes of contamination. Pests, insect bodies, droppings, eggs and nesting materials can all cause problems if you do not have effective pest control and cleaning regimes in place.

Keep food areas clean and clear and in good condition and report or deal with damage to equipment or premises immediately. Remove waste safely and hygienically regularly throughout the day, do not allow waste to build up. Report or deal with signs of pests immediately.

Chemical hazards

Chemicals which may be harmful, can accidentally be introduced to food in various ways and from different sources. There are chemical hazards from the environment which may be the product of industrial processing. There are also agricultural residues like pesticides, fertilisers, animal antibiotics and hormones. Food additives like colours, flavour enhancers and preservatives may also present chemical hazards if used incorrectly. Workplace practices could cause chemical contamination if products such as cleaners are not used correctly.

Symptoms of chemical contamination may include diarrhoea, abdominal pain and vomiting which may be very similar to those presented as a result of other types of food poisoning. However some chemical poisoning may take months or even years to develop as people might only digest a very small amount of the harmful chemical over a long period. Life threatening conditions can occur, including brain damage, kidney or liver failure and damage to the nervous system.

You are responsible for buying food from reputable suppliers, and for making checks for physical and chemical contaminants in food and ingredients. You also need to have in place appropriate measures for food safety within your premises to prevent physical or chemical contamination.

You should also have in place such processes as sieving, and washing, looking and checking for contaminants to protect the food you process. Work safely to avoid contamination from cleaning products. Report or deal with any hazards when they occur.

Biological hazards

These are the main cause of food poisoning. Bacteria are tiny life forms that live on, or in, our bodies and throughout the natural world. Biological food poisoning may also be caused by viruses, parasites and poisonous fish, plants or fungi.

Some useful terms
- **Binary Fission** - Bacterium multiply by splitting in two, this is called binary fission.
- **Bacteria** - single celled micro-organisms, too small to see. Even if food is heavily infected it may still be impossible to see, smell or taste that it is infected. Bacteria are found throughout the natural world and survive under many conditions. Not all bacteria is harmful and some are actually beneficial to humans and we would find it difficult to survive without them.
- **Helpful Bacteria** - sometimes known as 'friendly bacteria' help us grow crops and make foods like yoghurt and cheese. They help us digest food, we also use them to treat sewerage to make it safe, and to create medicines, laundry and cleaning products.
- **Pathogenic Bacteria** - A pathogen is an organism that causes disease. Pathogenic bacteria cause illnesses such as food poisoning.
- **Spoilage Bacteria** - make food perish quickly.
- **Spore** - the protective version of some bacteria. The spore helps the bacteria survive conditions such as cooking or drying.
- **Toxin** - a poison produced by some bacteria and moulds.

Pathogenic bacteria
Pathogenic, means 'disease causing' and these types of bacteria are responsible for most food related illnesses. Pathogenic bacterial contaminations come from many sources. Raw food, water, soil, people, air, dust, dirt, food waste, pets and pests are all sources of contamination.

As bacteria naturally exist in the environment, in water, soil and air as well as on, and in, animals, many raw foods are already contaminated with pathogenic bacteria before they reach your workplace. As food handlers, our bodies also carry bacteria. Pathogenic bacteria are spread by careless or inappropriate handling. Poor practices can introduce bacteria at numerous points in the food processing chain,

104

for example: hand washing, wrapping and covering, cleaning, storage, cooking, cooling and transportation.

Bacteria cannot travel very far on their own. Anything that helps bacteria travel is referred to as a 'vehicle of contamination'. Think about these as they are often involved in causing cross-contamination which may potentially result in food poisoning. In particular, the most common vehicles of contamination include hands, cleaning cloths, work surfaces, utensils and equipment.

Cross-contamination is when pathogenic bacteria are transferred from something, such as raw meats, carrying contamination onto other foods, often in a high risk group. High risk foods are typically ready-to-eat items that are ideal for bacteria to live on. These foods typically present the biggest potential food safety problems.

Spoilage bacteria
When food spoils and becomes unacceptable to eat it is referred to as decomposed, rotted, perished, deteriorated or simply gone bad. Moulds, yeasts and spoilage bacteria are the main causes. These bacteria are naturally present in the environment and can cause contamination in the same way as pathogenic bacteria. This type of spoilage damages the quality of food and reduces it's shelf life. In some instances it can also cause illness.

Bacterial reproduction
The reproduction of bacteria is referred to as multiplication. The bacteria divide by binary-fission (dividing in two) and requires only 10-20 minutes to multiply, given the right conditions. It may only take a few hours for bacteria to reach millions.

Viruses, parasites and other biological hazards
Fungi, moulds, viruses and parasites all present other biological hazards to food.

Viruses are tiny micro-organisms that are carried on food and in water, but they do not need food or moisture to survive.

Polluted water and sewerage present the most usual sources of contamination from viruses. They can contaminate any kind of food but they are most usually associated with water, food from water (like shellfish) and raw food like vegetables and salad leaves.

Viruses can be spread by humans as vehicles of contamination. Unwashed hands, for example, may be the vehicle by which a virus transfers from the human to the food.

Parasites are organisms that live in or on other organisms. For example, fleas on pets, roundworms, flatworms and flukes can be present in pork, beef and fish. Some microscopic types of these organisms may be present in water. Meat and fish must be cooked thoroughly to kill any parasites present in the raw food.

Natural poisons

Some foods are naturally poisonous to humans.
These include:
- Kidney beans until they have been cooked thoroughly.
- Certain parts of some fish.
- Some fungi.
- Rhubarb leaves.
- Treated fish that may not have been processed correctly.

If you are using these products, they should be bought from reliable sources and the food handlers should take appropriate precautions to make and keep them safe to eat.

Your responsibilities

Everyone who deals with food at any stage has the responsibility to stay alert to any risks, including biological, physical and chemical hazards to prevent contamination.

Always deal with or report any concerns you may have about food safety immediately. Maintain food preparation procedures that help to prevent cross-contamination and maintain food safety.

Keep a record of temperatures and cleaning procedures. Record any problems and how they are dealt with, should issues arise.

Illness from Food

Most illnesses linked with food are caused by bacteria. At the very least, they can cause discomfort. This section identifies the features of illnesses caused by biological contaminants and allergens.

Illnesses are caused in two ways:
- **Food poisoning:**
  Caused by eating food contaminated with pathogenic bacteria or harmful substances, moulds, or poisons.
- **Food-borne illness:**
  Created by harmful micro-organisms carried on the food consumed, this includes viruses, parasites and certain pathogenic bacteria.

A small number of individuals may also become ill due to allergens which they cannot tolerate.

Food Poisoning

Pathogenic bacteria most commonly involved with food poisoning include:
- Salmonella.
- Staphylococcus aureus.
- Clostridium perfringens.
- Bacillus cerus.

This kind of food poisoning usually results in illness due to the following circumstances:
- High risk foods becoming contaminated.
- Food is kept in unsuitable conditions that allow bacteria to multiply.
- Food undercooked, resulting in bacteria not being totally destroyed.
- Food infected with bacteria is eaten.

The bacteria can make a person ill with:
- Abdominal pain.
- Nausea.
- Feeling sick.

- Vomiting.
- Diarrhoea.
- Headache.
- Fever.

Most pathogenic bacteria start to make you feel ill around 8 to 36 hours after you have digested the contaminated food.

Certain bacteria like Staphylococcus aureus produce poison even before the food is digested. In these cases you are likely to feel ill quite soon after eating the food, possibly within 1 to 6 hours.

Some bacteria make you feel ill as a result of forming spores enabling the bacteria to survive harsh conditions like cooking.

Most of these illnesses will last for around 24 to 48 hours but they could last much longer. For some people, including those in 'at risk' groups, food poisoning could be life-threatening.

Food-borne illnesses

Food-borne illnesses are caused by micro-organisms that are carried by the food or drink that is consumed. Only a very small number of microbes may cause food-borne illnesses. It is very important to use reputable suppliers and for food handlers to use good food practises to keep food safe and avoid contamination.

Food-borne illness can be caused by the following bacteria:
- Campylobacter, this is one of the most common causes of illness from bacteria.
- Escherichia coli 0157 (E.coli).
- Listeria.
- Typhoid and dysentery causing bacteria.

Viruses such as Hepatitis and Norovirus can also be food-borne, as can parasites such as tapeworms. The symptoms of food-borne illness can be very similar to those of food poisoning. Some can lead to kidney failure, paralysis or even death.

It may take weeks or even months for symptoms to appear and

the illness may not be short lived and could have serious long term consequences for the individual concerned.

Food and bacteria links

The table below shows foodstuffs with particular links to bacterial contaminants

Type	Bacteria	Food typically linked
Food poisoning	Salmonella	Raw poultry, eggs, meats and raw milk
Food poisoning	Staphylococcus aurea	Cold meats, raw milk, dairy products and anything touched by hand
Food poisoning	Clostridium perfringens	Cooked meat and poultry
Food poisoning	Clostridium botulinum	Fish, meat, vegetables, smoked fish, canned fish and corned beef
Food poisoning	Bacillus cerus	Cereals
Food borne illness	Campylobacter jejuni	Raw poultry, meat, milk and un-treated water
Food borne illness	Escherichia coli 0157 (E.coli)	Beef (particularly minced), other meats, raw milk, untreated water
Food borne illness	Listeria	Soft cheese, salad vegetable, pate, cheese made from unpasteurised milk,
Food borne illness	Shigella (dysentery)	Water, milk, salad vegetables

People at Particular Risk

People may be at greater risk of food poisoning or food-borne illness if they are in one of the 'at risk' groups. These groups include the very young, the elderly, pregnant women and their unborn child and people who are ill, convalescing or infirm and those who have weakened immunity.

High Risk Foods

There are some food products that are more likely to cause food poisoning than others. This is because they provide ideal conditions for bacteria to multiply to a level that may cause illness.

As a food handler, you need to identify high risk foods so that you can take all necessary precautions to prevent them causing illness.

The most important things to remember regarding high-risk foods are:
- **Ready-to-eat foods:**
  As the name suggests, ready-to-eat food can be eaten straight away and without further preparation like washing or cooking. This makes this groups particularly vulnerable to bacterial growth.
- **High-risk foods provide ideal conditions for bacterial multiplication:**
  Food that is full of protein and are moist, make ideal conditions for bacteria to grow.
- **High-risk food requires strict time or/and temperature controls:**
  The temperature of high risk foods is critical. In particular, these foods should spend as little time as possible in warm conditions.

High risk foods may be of animal or vegetable origin, cooked or uncooked, and may be eaten cold or re-heated.

High risk foods include:
- Cooked meats and poultry.
- Cooked meat products like gravy, soups, stews, stocks etc.
- Meat and fish pate and spreads.
- Milk, eggs and dishes including uncooked or lightly cooked milk and eggs, like mayonnaise, hollandaise sauce and mousses.
- Shellfish and seafood including prawns, crab, oysters etc.
- Cooked rice.
- Delicatessen products.
- Prepared salads, leaves and vegetables.

Conditions for bacterial growth

The ideal conditions for bacterial multiplication are a combination of:
- Food.
- Moisture.
- Warmth.
- Time.

Food
All living things require nutrients and that includes bacteria. Different bacteria live on different foods but most require something which is high in protein. These protein-rich foods will allow bacteria to thrive and multiply quickly.

Moisture
Bacteria need moisture to stay alive and cannot multiply on dry food. However quantities of salt or sugar in foods like savoury biscuits, confectionery and jam, prevent bacteria from multiplying easily.

Warmth
Food poisoning bacteria and fungi multiply most effectively between 5°C and 63°C. This is referred to as the 'danger zone'. Ambient temperature is the term used to describe normal room temperature and this is generally within the danger zone. The ideal temperature for bacterial multiplication is 37°C which is the average human body temperature.

At temperatures below 5°C bacterial growth usually slows down or stops altogether. This is why fridges should be set between 0°C and 5°C. However most bacteria survive colder temperature and will be able to resume multiplication when the temperature rises again.

The food handler must bear this in mind when handling food from cold storage. Some bacteria, including Listeria, and some moulds, can multiply below 5°C so special attention is required with foods prone to these bacteria or moulds. Freezing may make most bacteria dormant but does not usually kill them. Multiplication will restart when the food is thawed.

Cooking at high temperatures kills most bacteria, providing the cooking is for long enough. Generally the thickest part of the food needs to be held above 70°C for at least two minutes,

Some bacteria produce spores and these can survive normal cooking temperatures. They develop a protective coating that helps them survive harsh conditions like high temperatures, dehydration and even disinfection. The bacteria do not multiply when they are in their spore state, but when conditions improve, the bacteria emerge and resume multiplication.

Common spore forming bacteria are Bacillus cereus, Clostridium perfringens and Clostridium botulinum.

Time
With the right conditions, bacteria need time to grow. 10-20 minutes is enough time to enable multiplication in the right conditions. One bacterium splits to become two, two become four, four become eight and so on, so it is easy to see that it does not take long for there to be enough pathogenic bacteria to cause food poisoning.

Other factors in bacterial growth
The level of acidity in food can affect multiplication. This is why vinegar is used in pickling.

The level of oxygen can effect multiplication of certain bacteria, though some can survive and multiply without the need for oxygen.

Handling high-risk foods

When dealing with high-risk foods all food handlers should:
- Avoid touching the food by hand and use tools wherever possible to avoid cross-contamination.
- Keep high-risk and raw foods apart at all times because raw foods are a major source of food poisoning bacteria.
- Cover food during storage to prevent cross-contamination.
- Keep food out of the danger zone (5^0C - 63^0C) during preparation, serving and sale.
- Hot-holding (for example of ready to serve meals), should be maintained at or above 63^0C.

Time and Temperature

Best practice

As a food handler you need to take control of the risk factors that may affect food that you are responsible for.

All food handlers must:
- Restrict the time that food remains at temperatures that are in the danger zone between 5°C and 63°C, the general rule is no more than 4 hours.
- Maintain low temperatures at 5°C or below, outside the danger zone to prevent bacterial growth, for example, freezing high-risk food.
- Use high temperatures above 63°C, outside the danger zone to kill bacteria by cooking thoroughly.

Food will pass through the danger zone but every care should be taken to restrict the time food spends between 5°C and 63°C. Some food products may pass through this temperature zone several times during preparation. Remember the times when food is left standing, on display, being delivered, stored, heated or cooled slowly.

Topping-up practices are discouraged as they prolong the time food remains at ambient temperatures - for example, when topping up hot foods.

Poor practice

Temperature and time are causes often linked to food illnesses. These problems are usually caused by:
- Cooling food too slowly before refrigeration.
- Leaving food at room temperature instead of refrigerating it.
- Preparing food too far ahead of sale or service and keeping it at ambient temperature.
- Under cooking meat and poultry.
- Thawing food insufficiently before cooking.
- Re-heating food inadequately.
- Hot-holding below 63°C allowing bacteria to multiply.

Because food may pass through the danger zone several times, it is vital that the time in the danger zone is restricted to a minimum.

High and low temperatures

Remember that low temperatures do not destroy bacteria. Low temperatures slow down the growth of most bacteria but some can continue to multiply, like Listeria. Most bacteria are not killed by freezing and some parasites can survive freezing for quite long periods of time.

Cooking at high temperature (70^0C or hotter) will destroy most pathogenic bacteria provided that the cooking is for long enough and reaches through to the thickest part of the food. Because some bacterial spores can withstand cooking, high temperature processes such as pasteurisation are used to make food safer. Commercial sterilisation and ultra-heat treatments are also used to help prolong the shelf life of some food products.

Keeping food safe

Keeping food out of the danger zone reduces the chances for bacterial growth. Food handlers need to control time and temperature at every stage using good practices.

- Ensure food arrives at your premises at the correct temperature. This should be between 0^0C and 5^0C for refrigerated items and between -22^0C and -18^0C for frozen foods and should be checked on every delivery.
- Refrigerate raw, highly perishable and high-risk foods immediately after delivery. Check the refrigerator temperature daily.
- Cook food thoroughly. Check that the core temperature of meat and poultry reaches 70^0C and is sustained for at least two minutes.
- Keep food refrigerated until just before preparation or serving. Check the temperature regularly in a cold-holding area, it should be between 0^0C and 5^0C.
- Serve hot food above 63^0C. Check temperature regularly in a

hot-holding area, it should be kept at or above 63⁰C.

- Cool food as rapidly as possible. Ideally cool to between 0⁰C and 5⁰C within one to two hours, checking the temperature once cooled.
- Thaw food by an approved method or as directed on packaging. Thawed food should be temperature checked and remain between 0⁰C and 5⁰C
- Re-heat food adequately. In England and Wales a core temperature of 70⁰C held for 2 minutes is required. In Scotland the minimum legal temperature for re-heating food is 82⁰C.
- Frozen food should remain below -18°C. Freezer temperature should be checked daily.

There are a range of temperature measuring devices on the market, from scanners, temperature probes and thermometers and integral equipment in fridges, freezers etc. Make sure you know how to use the correct device for measuring temperatures and that you understand what needs to be recorded and how to record it. Also determine procedures to deal with issues regarding unsafe temperature readings.

Your business and temperature control

It is important to understand that processes and temperature procedures may vary between food establishments. You will need to understand the procedures used or develop procedures that fit your purposes and keep food safe.

Within the business of cake decorating, temperature recording processes are minimal due to the lower risk of the food products you will be working with. You do not need to probe cakes for temperature checks and you will probably be very aware of your oven temperature.

You should however, regularly check refrigerator temperature and, if you freeze cakes and icings, your freezer. This is necessary to ensure food safety. Keep a log of temperature checks - this is included in the Safer Food Better Business pack (see page 77) which gives you a diary in which to record all necessary food business processes.

If you discover a temperature reading outside the acceptable range for your business, you must apply corrective procedures, report problems and actions taken and dispose of food if necessary.

Personal Hygiene

People are a common source of pathogenic bacteria, so maintaining a high standard of personal hygiene is essential for all food handlers. Maintaining good personal habits will help maintain safe food and avoid contamination and the risk of food illnesses.

A clean and tidy start for every day not only makes you feel good but will also give a good impression of your business. Regular washing removes some of the bacteria naturally present on skin as well as removing perspiration that bacteria thrive upon. Using deodorant helps to prevent body odour, but strong smelling perfumes and deodorants should be avoided because they can taint some foods.

Hand washing is vital for even the most healthy people. Hands potentially carry harmful bacteria and can easily transfer the contaminant to food. Try to avoid touching food with your bare hands - use tools or gloves where possible. Your hands will inevitably come in contact with utensils, equipments, surfaces, etc. and therefore must be kept clean at all times.

Hand washing helps to prevent food contamination and cross-contamination by your hands. It will help to remove pathogenic bacteria, parasites, viruses and any other harmful substances like dust and dirt.

When washing your hands you should always use a hand wash basin, specifically for this purpose and not a sink designed for food washing or washing up. A liquid hand cleaner is better than a bar of soap as it does not run the risk of carrying bacteria form the last person who used it. Rinse your hands well before drying and use paper towels or roller towels to dry your hands. Never use a tea towel or service cloth which may then transfer harmful substances to food.

Always wash your hands before starting work and before touching raw or high-risk food. Wash your hands as often as necessary when working with food and in particular, when switching between handling raw and cooked food. Always wash your hands after handling raw food, including eggs in their shells, carrying out cleaning tasks, visiting the toilet, sneezing, coughing, touching your hair or face, or dealing with rubbish. Eating, drinking and smoking are activities that should remain outside the food preparation area and you should wash your hands before returning to food preparation.

Do not wear nail varnish. It may chip and flake into food and it can also hide dirt. Nail varnish should be removed before handling food.

Staphylococcus aureus can be found on healthy people, particularly in cuts, spots and in other skin conditions. Any affected areas should always be covered with waterproof plaster. If the area is on your hands, you may need to wear gloves as well. Blue waterproof plasters are usually used in food establishments so that they are clearly visible if they should come off. If a plaster does fall off, appropriate action should be taken. If you have a septic or weeping cut or abrasion, tell your supervisor before you start work, or if you are the person in charge, you may need to consider staying away from food for a time.

Appropriate clothing

Clothing for a food business will depend upon the type of business carried out. Overalls, jackets, aprons, trousers, hair nets, non-slip shoes and gloves are all examples of items of clothing that may or may not be required for safe food handling. In some cases body-warmers may be required for work in cold environments.

Protective clothing is designed to protect food from contamination, it will also protect your own clothes. Protective clothing should be suitable to work in and be kept in good, clean condition. Light coloured clothing will allow dirt to show up, prompting changing and cleaning. It should be easy to clean.

Put on protective clothing before you enter the work environment and do not continue to wear protective clothing after exiting the food environment but remove it immediately. This will help to reduce the risk of contaminants getting into food areas.

You may need to wear a hat or hair net and this is common in many food premises. It should cover as much of your hair as possible. If you have long hair, it should be tied or pinned back. Beards and moustaches may also require covering. Never deal with your hair in the food environment and put on protective hair covering before you enter the food area. Do not wear outdoor clothing in a food premises and store outdoor clothing away from food areas.

Jewellery

Watches and all other jewellery should be left outside the food premises. Bacteria can live under straps and in and around chains. Gemstones and other small parts could drop into food. A plain wedding band is allowed and sometimes sleeper earings but some food establishments may require these to be covered (by a plaster).

Unhygienic habits

These habits often go unnoticed and may seem harmless but pathogens can spread very easily if they go unchecked.

- Do not forget to wash your hands before handling food and between handling raw and cooked food.
- Never forget to wash your hands after going to the toilet or dealing with rubbish.
- Never dry your hands on your apron, tea towel or serving cloth.
- Never pick your nose or wipe your nose on your sleeve.
- Do not cough, sneeze or spit over food.
- Do not blow or breathe onto glass to polish it.
- Do not blow onto food to remove dust or to cool it.
- Never lick your fingers or use them to taste food.
- Always use a clean spoon when tasting food.
- Never eat, drink or smoke in a food area.

Illness

You must not work with food if you have certain illnesses or symptoms because you could contaminate food. It is a legal requirement to report certain illnesses to health authorities and you or your employer should ensure that this is done where appropriate. Obviously you should seek medical attention when necessary and you may need a doctor's approval before resuming work with food.

You must inform your employer (if you have one) if you are suffering from diarrhoea, vomiting, nausea, ear, nose or eye discharges and any septic or weeping wounds and skin conditions. You must also report any food poisoning conditions suffered by close family and friends as you could become a carrier. Carriers can unknowingly contaminate food without becoming ill themselves.

You or your employer will decide what to do. You may need to see a doctor who will need to know that you are a food handler and will then advise whether further tests are necessary. You, your employer or your doctor will advise on when you can return to work.

Premises and Equipment

Your premises needs to be maintained for food safety, and your equipment also needs to be organised and maintained with food safety in mind. It may be your responsibility or the responsibility of your employer to ensure that your workplace remains well organised and you will need to be aware of the general principles involved to help you maintain high standards in the premises, regarding equipment, utensils and food areas.

The premises needs to be fit for purpose. It must be suitable for the type of food business carried out. The design, construction and equipping of the premises should minimise the risks to food. Some important considerations include the ability to facilitate a safe work-flow particularly regarding raw and cooked foods where appropriate. The premises needs to allow suitable temperature controls and reduce the risk of contamination to food. It needs suitable ventilation, clean water, food storage, staff cleaning facilities, waste disposal, pest control, and allow for ease of cleaning.

All of the considerations mentioned above will help you to produce a safe environment in which to prepare food and control the risks from food hazards.

Construction

Surfaces, walls, floors and ceilings should be smooth and without cracks. Light coloured materials make it easier to see dirt. It helps if ceilings and floors are grease resistant and coving on the joins between ceilings and walls can help make cleaning easier. Windows and doors should have screens or strip curtains (if appropriate) to reduce contamination. There should be no flaking paint. Where appropriate, non-slip floors and fire retardant materials should be used to create an environment that is safe for workers as well as food production.

The construction design should allow for work-flow that protects food from contamination from the moment it is delivered to the premises until the moment it leaves. Work-flow is the route the food takes through your premises. Try to have a storage area near to where deliveries are received so that they are not carried through the premises. Preparation could start near the relevant storage area and then progress logically through the premises to an area suitable for packaging for final delivery, sale or service. Washing up and food washing facilities should be well away from food service and sale or where it is consumed. Raw and ready-to-eat foods should be kept apart.

As a food handler you will play an important part in organising and maintaining a safe work-flow for food in the premises. All parts of the building construction must be maintained in good condition to prevent physical contamination of food.

Materials and equipment

Food equipment and utensils, including surfaces, are best made from durable, easy to clean materials. Smooth surfaces are more resistant to cracking and chipping and they will be easier to clean. All utensils, surfaces and equipments must be made from non-toxic, non-porous, rust resistant material. Make sure crockery, pots and pans are also free of cracks and chips that can harbour bacteria and be harder to clean. Use colour coded equipment if it is provided to keep raw and processed foods separate.

Equipment should be easy to clean. Equipment that is not built in, should be mobile to allow cleaning of all areas.

You must have enough refrigerator space to be able to store cooked and uncooked food separately. If you do not have separate refrigerators extra care must be taken to keep food safe.

All equipment and utensils must be maintained in good condition to prevent physical contamination of food.

Facilities and services

Lighting, ventilation, hot water, toilets and hand wash basins must be provided for staff use. Hand wash basins should be separate from food washing facilities and have hot and cold running water, preferably with wrist or foot operated taps to prevent cross-contamination. Liquid soap should be provided, and drying paper or roller towels supplied for hand drying.

Never wash food at a hand wash basin and never wash hands at a food washing sink as this could cause the spread of bacteria.

A first aid box should be provided within easy reach of workers. It should include brightly coloured waterproof plasters. First aid equipment should be marked with a white cross on a green background.

Cleaning and Disinfection

There is an expectation from consumers that food premises will be clean. This also creates a good impression and makes for a safe environment for food preparation and for everyone who works there. Although everything may look clean, this does not necessarily mean that it is not contaminated. Every food premises should follow general guidelines regarding cleaning and disinfection.

The aim of cleaning is to protect food from contamination by reducing the opportunities for bacterial multiplication as well as protecting from physical and chemical contamination. Cleaning will help to prevent pests and maintain a safe environment for workers.

By carrying out necessary cleaning and disinfection, food businesses will uphold their legal and moral obligation to keep food safe.

Disinfectants
Disinfection reduces bacteria to a safe level and this can be achieved with very hot water (above 82^{0}C) steam or with the use of chemical disinfectants. Heat can be combined with chemical disinfectants. The chemical reduces pathogenic micro-organisms to a level that will safeguard health. They kill all bacteria and cannot kill spore creating bacteria.

Disinfectants must be used after initial cleaning so that they will work properly. Follow the directions provided with the disinfectant as they need to be left on the surface long enough to work properly. The required contact time will be specified in the individual products' instructions.

Detergents
These help to dissolve grease and remove dirt but they will not kill all bacteria. The combination of detergent and hot water, and the action of cleaning will kill some pathogenic bacteria, but most will survive. Therefore to prevent bacteria from causing illness, there may be some cause for disinfecting after the items have been cleaned.

Sanitisers
Sanitisers combine the job of a detergent and a disinfectant, provided the instructions are followed properly. Sanitisers may be used instead of detergents and disinfectants.

Where to use disinfectant

What and when to disinfect will depend largely upon quantity and type of use. Surfaces and equipment that come into contact with food, especially raw and high-risk food, and pieces of equipment and surfaces that are frequently handled are at serious risk of cross-contamination. They should be washed after every use and between uses where necessary.

This includes the need to disinfect/sanitise things that come into contact with food like chopping boards, surfaces, work boards, food processors, mixers, slicers, cooking utensils and containers etc. Disinfection/sanitizing should include things which come into contact with hands like door handles, cupboards, fridges, freezers and window handles, taps and switches, and finally any contamination hazards like waste bins (including the lids), mops and cloths.

It is best and most efficient to clean as you go. Things like chopping boards and utensils should cleaned and disinfected immediately after every use, most particularly when dealing with raw or high-risk and ready-to-eat foods.

Some areas of the premises will be cleaned less often, but at frequent intervals. It is best to have a schedule for cleaning that includes daily, weekly and monthly tasks. Floors and bins probably need doing daily but cleaning under fridges and movable appliances is possibly required once a week with high level cleaning once a month or quarterly.

Your employer or yourself, if you own the business, are responsible for a proper cleaning schedule, that should be laid out as a clear timetable. This timetable should set out when, but also how, specific cleaning tasks should be carried out. It may also state what products should be used and who should do it. It can also include details of other parties, if relevant, for dealing with things like dismantling machinery for cleaning, dealing with hazardous chemicals, pest control company details, etc.

Cleaning processes

Surfaces

When cleaning surfaces make sure all food is protected from contamination. Remove any loose dirt and wash the surface with hot water and detergent, using a cloth, or scourer. Rinse off the detergent with a clean cloth and use a chemical disinfectant, following the manufacturers instructions and ensuring the required contact time. Rinse surfaces with clean water and allow to air dry or dry with disposable paper towels.

Washing-up

Dishwashers may clean and disinfect effectively with rinse temperatures over 74^{0}C but commonly household dishwashers may only reach temperatures of 49^{0}C to 60^{0}C, sufficient to allow bacterial growth and even promote it. Some models have high temperature or sterilization settings but only commercial models will definitely reach high enough temperatures to reliably disinfect and sterilise.

It is not necessary to have a commercial dishwasher for a home cake decorating business. Many items for this type of business will have to be washed by hand. If possible it is best to have two sinks alongside each other.

Wear gloves to protect hands from heat and chemicals. Remove any food particles before washing and then wash at about 55^{0}C with detergent and a cloth, brush or scourer. Change the water if it becomes too cool or dirty. Rinse items in very hot water (over 80^{0}C is recommended) and leave to soak for at least 30 seconds to kill bacteria. It is best to leave items to air dry in a clean area away from contamination.

The six stages of cleaning

1. **Prepare** - remove loose food, soak as necessary.
2. **Clean** - wash with detergent (if using sanitizer go next to step 5).
3. **Rinse** - remove all trace of detergent.
4. **Disinfect** - following instructions for contact time.
5. **Final rinse** - with clean hot water.
6. **Dry** - air dry if possible (fabric cloths must be cleaned frequently and used for one batch of drying only).

Cloths and cleaning equipment

Because cloths and tea-towels etc. can become contaminated with bacteria and microscopic organisms, single-use disposable cloths and towels are recommended. Never use cloths in food areas that have been used for cleaning, of any sort. Where you use cloths for washing up, replace them with clean ones regularly. Never use service cloths or oven gloves for drying your hands.

Disinfect and clean mops and cloths frequently, leaving them to air dry. Following manufacturer's instructions when using disinfectant.

Store cleaning equipment, chemicals and protective clothing away from food areas.

Sterilising

Sterilisation is the process of destroying all pathogens and spoilage organisms. It is not usually possible, or necessary, to sterilise food premises, particularly a home baking business. You will most commonly find sterilisation used in medical environments.

Bins and rubbish

You will need to have bins near food areas, but try to keep them far enough removed to prevent contamination. Bins should be regularly cleaned and have a bin liner. Lids which do not require hand operation will reduce risk of cross-contamination. You will also need outside bins and these should have well fitting lids and liners. If possible, have foot operated lids to help you avoid hand contact.

Always remove securely tied bags of rubbish from bins in the food areas to outside bins when they become full, but at least every day. Clean indoor bins at the end of the day or work period. Keep bin areas inside and outside, neat, clean and tidy to discourage pests. Always wash your hand after handling bins or rubbish.

Pests

Typically, food pests live in, on and around food and humans. The most common include insects, rodents, birds and stored food pests such as weevils and beetles. These all present a risk of contamination to food and there have been cases of food poisoning resulting from a food handlers contact with animals, for example, pets, before handling food.

Food, moisture, warmth and shelter are all present in the food premises and this provides the ideal environment for pests, giving them all they need to survive. Ensuring doors and windows are kept closed or screened, will reduce the likelihood of pests entering the food area. Ensure walls and floors are crack free and you do not have gaps around skirtings, windows and pipes etc.

Many pests will inhabit unhealthy places where they will pick up pathogenic bacteria, for example, rats in sewers and flies on rubbish. Some pests will carry pathogenic bacteria within them and their droppings or saliva can transfer the bacteria. Pests can also spread food-borne diseases like dysentery and illnesses like Weil's disease through contaminated water.

Pests also present a physical hazard if their bodies, droppings, eggs or even nesting materials get into food. Pest infestations can cause diseases through food poisoning and food-borne illnesses, but also cause damage to your business's reputation and profit. Damage may be caused to the physical structure of buildings, equipment or cables and pipes. This may result in increased risks, for example tripping, slipping, flooding and fire hazards.

Non-compliance with the law to keep food safe, can result in fines, court cases or even closure of the business.

You or your employer are responsible for ensuring that pests do not present a hazard to food within your premises. You or you employer should make sure necessary measures are put in place to ensure that food is kept safe from contamination at all times. Never leave food uncovered, check all deliveries, check and rotate stored goods, maintain bin areas, keep doors, windows and screens closed.

Maintain the premises with clean, undamaged and crack-free surfaces, equipment and building structure. Deal with any issues that may present a risk from pests quickly and efficiently.

Prevention is always better than cure, so watch out for sign of pests and deal with any signs as soon as they are spotted. If necessary, you may need to involve pest controllers. Most infestations can be treated effectively with baited traps, pesticides and insecticides but make sure you follow directions carefully. Electric ultra-violet fly killers are an effective control in food environments but must also be cleaned regularly to remove dead insects.

Storage

Food storage is an important part of any catering business, and those who handle food should have some training. Keeping food safe involves maintaining the best conditions for food at various stages in the production of the final product. Food handlers have a legal responsibility to do everything possible to protect food and keep it safe. It is illegal to sell spoilt food.

Hazardous and/or inedible substances must be labelled adequately and stored in secure containers away from food areas.

If working from your home, you will need separate places to store food for your business. Your refrigerated goods should also be kept separate to maintain total control on food prepared by your business. Dairy products, cooked products and prepared ready-to-eat uncooked food and items marked 'keep refrigerated', must be stored and transported below 8°C, but above 5°C or lower. You should check the temperature of the refrigerator at least once a day.

Keep checks on products marked with 'use-by' dates and use a strict rotation system to organise the use of food products and ingredients. You must store raw materials and all ingredients in appropriate conditions, designed to prevent harmful deterioration and protect them from contamination.

Preservation processes may be used to keep food fresh longer. Heat treatment, freezing, drying, chemical preservation, smoking and vacuum packing are examples of preservation processes that might be used. Once the packaging of preserved foods is broken, the contents must be treated as if they were fresh.

Key words
These terms relate to the storage and care of all food items that you may be responsible for:
- **Shelf-life**:
    Indicates the period of time food can be stored (in the correct manner for the food stuff)and still be maintained in a safe and good condition.

- **Date Marks**:
    Refers to use-by, best-before and other date terms used to indicate when food is safe.
- **Use-by Date**:
    Date displayed on highly perishable food indicating the safe period when food remains in the best condition.
- **Best-before Date**:
    Date displayed on less perishable food such as frozen dried and canned foods, indicating a recommended storage life.

Date marks help to identify foods that may not visibly appear spoiled. Date marks are a legal requirement. In the UK we currently use 'best-before' and 'use-by'.

It is against the law to change the date markings unless the food is re-treated or processed in a way that will increase the shelf life of the food, maintaining it in good condition.

Receiving deliveries

Do not accept raw materials or ingredients or any other materials if they might be contaminated in a way that means the final product would be unfit for human consumption.

You or someone in your business must be responsible for the checking of all deliveries. The person responsible should check the dates, packaging, temperature, appearance and any presence of pests in all deliveries. You may reject food deliveries because of damaged packaging, or because it is thawed or not refrigerated to the right temperature. It may be infested with pests, or show signs of mould or other spoilage. Check and return dented or rusty cans, and items that are outside their safe date marks.

Do not accept products without the correct paperwork. Inadequate paperwork will leave you without clear traceability from food source to your business. Try to manage all deliveries as they arrive i.e. do not let deliveries pile up, unsorted. Perishables need to be put into the correct storage as soon as they arrive to uphold your food hygiene standards. Removing packaging from your work area will stop any chance of cross-contamination.

Storage guidelines

Follow any guidelines on food products for storage, regarding temperature, packaging etc. Ensure you always use appropriate stock rotation. Make sure the products with the shortest shelf life are used first. Check the date marks of products before you use them.

Make sure foods that require cold storage are stored correctly in the fridge or freezer. Eggs should be stored in the refrigerator when there is space and no risk of contamination. Otherwise eggs should be kept in a cold store room. Some fruit and vegetables may also be stored in the fridge but must be cleaned and stored separately from other foods.

As a home business you will probably be running one general purpose fridge. Your fridge temperature should be set between 0^0C and 5^0C. Always store raw meat and poultry on a shelf below other foods to reduce the risk of dripping onto other foods and contaminating them. Stack fridge shelves so that cold air can circulate freely and you can easily check the stock. Avoid leaving the fridge door open longer than necessary. Never put hot food into the fridge as this will raise the temperature and produce condensation, causing dripping over other foods.

Your freezer temperature should be -18^0C or below. This will prevent micro-organisms from multiplying and they will remain dormant. Do not re-freeze frozen food once de-frosted and make sure food in properly de-frosted before being cooked or processed as necessary before serving.

Put raw food below high-risk food as you would in the fridge, to reduce risk of contamination. Do not put unwrapped food in the freezer and make sure foods are well labelled and dated. Check packaging for signs of damage and rotate produce as you would in your store cupboard or fridge.

Make sure all your storage areas are included in your cleaning programme.

Principles for Safe Preparation of Food

Principles of good preparation practise protect food from contamination at all times, and include:
- Wearing protective clothing and washing your hands regularly.
- Touching food as little as possible.
- Using the correct tools and utensils for the task in hand.
- Cleaning equipment, washing and disinfecting as necessary between processes.
- Ensuring temperature and time controls are adhered to in order to keep high-risk foods out of the danger zone.
- Using a clean spoon for tasting, each time it is required.
- Planning your preparation processes to allow plenty of time for processes like thawing or cooling.

Thawing and cooling of hot foods

Thawing and cooling are major processes frequently involved in food poisoning cases.

- Plan your time to take cooling and thawing into consideration.
- Protect cooling or thawing food from contamination.
- Use cooling and thawing methods appropriate to your workplace and food products.
- Keep cooling times as short as possible.

Cooling
Because hot food has to pass through the danger zone to cool, it must be cooled as quickly as possible to reduce the time spent in the danger zone. Protect the food from contamination during the cooling process and check the temperature of the food as it cools. The aim is to reduce the temperature to 5^0C as quickly as possible and ideally within two hours.

Without a blast chiller you will have to use one or more of the following methods.
- Divide the food into smaller portions.

- Put the food in shallow containers to spread it to allow it to cool more quickly.
- Use an ice bath. Transferring the food to cooler containers and immersing them in ice water will aid cooling.
- Stir frequently to aid cooling.
- You may be able to add ice to your food to help cool it quickly.

Thawing
It is unsafe to thaw high risk foods at an ambient temperature because it is in the danger zone.

Depending upon your food business and the type and size of the food products, you should use one of the following methods to thaw food:
- In a fridge at 5^0C or below.
- In a microwave oven following the manufacturers instructions.
- Submerged in cold running drinking water.

You should ensure thawing times are planned for. Make sure thawing foods do not present a risk to other foods (by dripping or overflowing juices for instance), placing thawing food in a fridge, below other foods. Cover food while it is thawing and make sure you select the most appropriate method to thaw each food item. Never re-freeze frozen food.

Cooking

Most bacteria are destroyed at temperatures of 70^0C and above. Cooking food until the core temperature is 75°C or above for at least two minutes, will ensure that harmful pathogenic micro-organisms are destroyed. Some businesses may have a policy to use a higher temperature for some foods. In some cases a lower cooking temperature is acceptable as long as the core temperature is maintained for a specified period of time.

The guidelines are as follows :
- 60°C for a minimum of 45 minutes.
- 65°C for a minimum of 10 minutes.
- 70°C for a minimum of 2 minutes.

Re-heating food

This is another common cause of food poisoning and many companies will ban re-heating entirely for this reason.

Rice is particularly high risk as the spores of the bacterium Bacillus cereus may germinate and produce a toxin, and if the rice is re-heated inadequately, this toxin may not be destroyed. If you do re-heat food, never do it more than once and discard any left-overs after use.

Remove food from the fridge only just before re-heating and serving and not any earlier making sure it is heated to at least 70°C (in Scotland this is 82°C) and maintain this for at least two minutes.

Hot and cold-holding and displaying food

Hot-holding must be maintained above 63°C. This ensures the food is kept outside the danger zone.

Cold-holding must be below 5°C keeping food at a temperature below the danger zone.

Check the temperature regularly to ensure food remains outside the danger zone. Displayed food should always be protected from contamination and be kept at the correct temperature for the food with regular checks.

Businesses that display food should have methods and systems in place to keep food safe while being displayed. Utensils and protective covers may be needed for serving areas and these should be regularly cleaned. Displayed food must be clearly labelled.

Chapter 7

Food Labelling and Packaging

Where labelling is appropriate make sure descriptions are clear and not misleading. Inspectors will look at how you describe food, for example on your labels, to make sure that descriptions are not misleading for customers.

More information on food safety labelling (including allergy) can be found at https://www.gov.uk. Further information can be found on the Food Standards Agency website http://www.food.gov.uk.

If you package food yourself, you must use packaging that is suitable for food use. Suitable packaging is marked 'for food contact' or has a symbol on it that looks like a wine glass and a fork.

There are special rules for using plastics, ceramics or cellophane for packaging. You must have written evidence that you have kept to them. This is known as a 'declaration of compliance' and you can get it from your packaging supplier.

You also need a 'declaration of compliance' if you buy food that's already packaged for sale in any of those materials.

Selling packaged food and drink products

The labels on all food products that are for sale must be:

- Clear and easy to read.
- Permanent.
- Easy to understand.
- Easily visible.
- Not misleading.

You must show certain basic information and list the ingredients. You might also have to show certain warnings. 'NOTES A' on the following page lays out what wording should be used.

Products sold loose or in catering businesses

If you run a catering business, you sell food loose or package it for sale in your shop, (this includes decorated cakes and edible sugarcraft) you only need to show:

- The name of the food.
- If any of the ingredients have been irradiated, or have come from genetically modified sources.
- Certain warnings - see 'NOTES A' next page
- Any food additive you have added.
- Allergen information - see 'NOTES B' on the following page.

NOTES A: Food and drink warnings

If your food contains certain ingredients listed below, you must show an appropriate warning on the label.

Ingredient	Wording you must use
Allura red (E129)	'May have an adverse effect on activity and attention in children'.
Aspartame	'Contains a source of phenylalanine'.
Caffeine over 150 mg/l	'Not suitable for children, pregnant women and persons sensitive to caffeine'.
Carmoisine (E122)	'May have an adverse effect on activity and attention in children'.
Liquorice	'Contains liquorice' (for confectionery or alcohol containing liquorice, extra wording may be needed).
Polyols	'Excessive consumption may cause a laxative effect'.
Ponceau 4R (E124)	'May have an adverse effect on activity and attention in children'.
Quinoline yellow (E104)	'May have an adverse effect on activity and attention in children'.
Raw milk	'This milk has not been heat-treated and may therefore contain organisms harmful to health'.
Skimmed milk with non-milk fat	There is no fixed wording, but you must show a warning that the product is unfit or not to be used for babies.
Sulphur dioxide over 10mg/l	'Contains sulphur dioxide (or sulphites/sulfites)'.
Sunset yellow (E110)	'May have an adverse effect on activity and attention in children'.
Sweeteners	'With sweetener(s)'.
Sweeteners and sugar	'With sugar and sweetener(s)'.
Tartrazine (E102)	'May have an adverse effect on activity and attention in children'.

Cake and confectionery labelling

Generally, cakes are not required to be labelled. However, if you choose to do so you must ensure that the description is true and accurate.

It is important to understand the difference between the words **'flavoured'** and **'flavour'**. As an example, vanilla **flavoured** butter-cream will derive it's flavour only from real vanilla, but vanilla **flavour** buttercream is synthetically flavoured. Where the description only reads 'vanilla buttercream' for example, the flavour must come only from natural vanilla.

The cream in cream cakes must be wholly dairy cream. If any artificial or imitation cream is used, the name of the cake must be qualified accordingly. Imitation cream must not be described as cream or crème. Similarly imitation chocolate must not be described as chocolate or choc.

Additives in cakes

If cakes contain any additive of the types listed on the previous page, then there must be a specific notice on them. The notice should clearly and conspicuously tell the customers which particular additives are present in those particular cakes.

Otherwise the shop must display a general notice in a prominent position near the food, telling customers that cakes sold there may contain such additives.

An example notice might say:

Food Labelling Regulations 1996.

Customers are advised that some of the cakes and flour confectionery sold on these premises may contain one, or more, of the following types of additives:

Antioxidants, Flavour Enhancers, Sweeteners, Colours Flavourings, Preservatives.

Chapter 8

Training

Training is available for many different aspects of running a business, including management, food preparation and specialist cake decorating courses.

Food safety

Keep up to date with food safety training. Food hygiene courses are designed to equip you with skills and knowledge to prepare and handle food hygienically. The Food Hygiene level 2 (CIEH) course is a recognised minimum requirement for anyone handling food. It is approved by the Chartered Institute of Environmental Health and meets the requirements of the Food Safety Act 1990 and the Food Safety Regulations 1995. It is advisable to refresh your training every three years.

Bookkeeping, accountancy and management

You may also choose to do accounting, bookkeeping or management courses, or you may need to look in to sending staff on these courses. You may be entitled to grants or loans for training and any costs that are incurred can be offset against your tax liability. The FSA has much information and guidance on starting a food business and your local authority may provide training courses.

More information is available about suitable business and food courses from your local authority, local library or further education college. You can also find details about further training through the Awarding Bodies for food safety training on the internet. A list of Awarding Bodies and their contact details is provided at the back of this book.

Baking and sugarcraft

Cake making is a popular business, so to compete, you'll need to make your cakes look as professional as possible. Training in aspects of the industry, including sugarcraft, marzipan techniques, chocolate work or blown sugar may be essential if you want to compete in an increasingly busy marketplace.

Part-time and full-time courses are available at educational establishments, covering all aspects of cake decorating and design. However many smaller sugarcraft schools offer short courses which may be invaluable if you cannot afford to spend the time or money on a full-time or longer courses.

There are various qualifications from NVQs to City and Guilds and diploma courses and some are becoming, to a certain degree, recognised in the industry.

Some diploma courses are run by sugarcraft companies and some by educational establishments, but there is no special or specific requirement for qualifications to be able to run a successful cake decorating business. You will find many a successful cake decorating business, run by individuals with no specific sugarcraft qualifications but with ample skill and ability. Much is learnt on the job and it is only in more recent times that sugarcraft qualifications have become readily available.

There are hundreds of courses available for all levels, you only have to search the Internet. For example, The Cake Makery run an extensive selection of courses for all abilities and in many different areas of the cake decorating business. These courses are aimed at increasing skill levels and provide an excellent way of improving just those skills you need to develop without the commitment or expense of a much longer course which may cover many things you already know.

Take time to consider where you put your time, energy and money to obtain the best and most suitable results to benefit your business. It should not be difficult to find one which will suit your requirements. Remember, this need not be for a particular named award, but to develop particular skills and abilities.

If you do achieve an NVQ, City & Guilds or a Diploma, this does not in any way guarantee you a wonderfully successful business. That will probably come from you personally, it will show in your style and that is what will get you noticed.

Cake decorating and sugarcraft courses can cost from a few pounds, to hundreds of pounds depending upon the level, length and the provider.

Some courses are available as downloadable files or software from the Internet that you can work through at your own pace. Others may be full-time classroom courses, short evening or day courses or apprenticeships.

It is worth shopping around and thinking carefully about your needs before committing to a course to make sure that you pick the right one for you or your staff.

Joining a sugarcraft club is another very good and fairly cheap way of picking up skills, hints and tips. The British Sugarcraft Guild at www.bsguk.org or The National Sugar Art Association at: www.nationalsugarartassociation.org.uk, both have branches across the UK where sugarcrafters meet regularly for demonstrations, workshops and exhibitions.

Both these sugarcraft organisations offer a wealth of knowledge in an informal, non-competitive environment, useful for asking questions and picking up many useful hints, tips and new ideas. There are sometimes other perks, like insurance deals, that come with membership to some organisations.

Chapter 9

Employing Staff

Parts of this chapter will already have been covered under other sections in this guide but they are also relevant here.

Legal requirements

You have certain legal requirements when employing staff.

There are no restrictions on staff numbers but if you employ staff you:
- Must agree a contract of employment.
- Will be required to deduct PAYE (Pay As You Earn) tax from wages.
- Are responsible for paying PAYE to the HMRC every month.
- Have to complete PAYE paperwork for your employees and a PAYE annual return each year.
- Need to complete relevant paperwork when a staff member leaves your employment and this includes providing form P45 to the employee when they leave.
- Are responsible for your employees' Class 1 National Insurance contributions .
- Are responsible for your employer contributions calculated as a percentage of an employee's wage.
- Are responsible for providing statutory sick pay when required.

The Contract

(This information is available on https://www.gov.uk website)
You will need to consider employment terms so that you can provide a contract of employment for each employee.

The contract is an agreement that sets out an employee's:
- Employment conditions.
- Employee rights.
- Employee responsibilities.
- Employee duties.

The sections of the contract will cover sick pay provision, equal opportunities, health and safety conditions, and together form the 'terms' of the contract.

Employees and employers must stick to a contract until it ends. It may end due to the employer or the employee giving notice or an employee being dismissed or until the terms are changed (usually by agreement between the employee and employer).

Note: If a person has an agreement to do some work for someone for example icing a Christmas cake for a customer, this is not an employment contract but a 'contract to provide services'.

Accepting a contract

An employment contract does not have to be written down.
As soon as someone accepts a job offer they have a contract with their employer.

Contract terms

The legal parts of a contract are known as 'terms'. An employer should make clear which parts of a contract are legally binding, e.g. an employer must pay employees at least the National Minimum Wage.

The contract terms could be:
- In written form, or similar document like a written statement of employment.
- Verbally agreed.
- In an employee handbook or on a company notice board.
- In an offer letter from the employer.
- Negotiated (or collective) agreements between employers and trade unions or staff associations.
- Automatically part of a contract (implied terms) even if they're not written down.

Examples of an implied term include:
- Employees not stealing from their employer.
- Employers providing a safe and secure working environment.
- A legal requirement such as the right to a minimum of 5.6 weeks' paid holidays.
- Something necessary to do the job, like a driver having a valid licence.
- Something that's been done regularly in a company over a long time like paying a Christmas bonus.

If there is nothing clearly agreed between you and your employee about a particular issue, it may be covered by an implied term.

Written Statement of Employment Particulars

An employer must give employees a 'written statement of employment particulars' if their employment contract lasts at least a month or more. This is not an employment contract but will include the main conditions of employment. The employer must provide the written statement within two months of the start of employment.

If an employee works abroad for more than a month during their first two months' employment, the employer must give them the written statement before they leave.

A written statement can be made up of more than one document. If this does happen, one of the documents (called the 'principal statement') must include as a minimum:
- The business's name.
- The employee's name, job title or description of work.

- Start date.
- If a previous job counts towards a period of continuous employment, the date the period started.
- How much and how often an employee will get paid.
- Hours of work (and if employees will have to work Sundays, nights or overtime).
- Holiday entitlement (and if that includes public holidays).
- Where an employee will be working and whether they might have to relocate.
- If an employee works in different places, where these will be and what the employer's address is.

As well as the principal statement, a written statement must also contain information about:
- How long a temporary job is expected to last.
- The end date of a fixed-term contract.
- Notice periods.
- Collective agreements.
- Pensions.
- Who to go to with a grievance.
- How to complain about how a grievance is handled.
- How to complain about a disciplinary or dismissal decision.

What a written statement does not need to include (but it must say where the information can be found):
- Sick pay and procedures.
- Disciplinary and dismissal procedures.
- Grievance procedures.

Statutory Sick Pay

(This information is available on HMRC's website).
Statutory Sick Pay (SSP) is paid to employees if they are unable to work because of illness. SSP is paid at the same time and in the same way as you would pay wages for the same period.

As an employer you're responsible for operating the SSP scheme, which includes making payments to employees who meet certain qualifying conditions (The weekly rate of SSP for days of sickness from 6 April 2013 is £86.70 for up to 28 weeks).

You must put your sickness policy in a written statement of employment particulars and give a copy to all employees who have worked for you for at least a month.

If you keep paying your employees their normal wage when they're sick - and you pay them at least as much as the SSP they are entitled to - you don't have to operate the SSP scheme.

You're only responsible for paying SSP if:
- You pay Class 1 National Insurance contributions for your employee (or would do if not for their age or their level of earnings).
- You don't provide your own occupational sick pay scheme.
- Your employee was sick for four or more days in a row (including non-working days).
- Your employee has told you they're sick within your own time limit (or seven days if you don't have one).

To qualify for Statutory Sick Pay (SSP) employees must:
- Have an employment contract.
- Have done some work under their contract.
- Have been sick for four or more days in a row (including non-working days) - known as a 'period of incapacity for work'.
- Earn at least £109 a week.
- Give you the correct notice.
- Give you proof of their illness, only after seven days off.

Employees who have been paid less than eights weeks of earnings still qualify for SSP. There is a sick pay calculator on www.gov.uk to calculate how much to pay them.

Employees can qualify for sick pay from more than one job. They could also qualify in one job but be fit for work in another, e.g. if one job is physical work that they can't do while ill but the other is office-based. If you have a high proportion of your workforce off sick at the same time you may be able to recover some or all of the SSP you pay from HMRC.

Employers liability insurance

(This information is available on the www.hse.gov.uk website).
Most employers are required by the law to insure against liability for
injury or disease to their employees arising from their employment.

Employers are responsible for the health and safety of their
employees while they are at work. Your employees may be injured
at work or they, or your former employees, may become ill as a
result of their work while in your employment. They might try to claim
compensation from you if they believe you are responsible.

The Employers' Liability (Compulsory Insurance) Act 1969 ensures that
you have at least a minimum level of insurance cover against any
such claims. Employers' liability insurance will enable you to meet the
cost of compensation for your employees' injuries or illness whether
they are caused on or off site. However, any injuries and illness relating
to motor accidents that occur while your employees are working for
you may be covered separately by your motor insurance.

Public liability insurance is different. It covers you for claims made
against you by members of the public or other businesses, but not
for claims by employees. While public liability insurance is generally
voluntary, employers' liability insurance is compulsory. You can be
fined if you do not hold a current employers' liability insurance policy
which complies with the law.

Under the law in Great Britain you do not need employers' liability
insurance to cover any of your employees who are based abroad
(e.g. if they are on secondment). However, you should check
whether the law in the country where they are based requires you
to take out insurance or take any other measures to protect your
employees.

Health and safety responsibilities

Employers have responsibilities for the health and safety of their
employees. They are also responsible for any visitors to their premises
such as customers, suppliers and the general public.
The Health and Safety at Work Act 1974 is the primary piece of

legislation covering work-related health and safety in the United Kingdom. It sets out a lot of your employers' responsibilities for your health and safety at work.

If you are employing staff you must you must carry out a health and safety risk assessment in the workplace and take action to remove any hazards. An employer has to appoint a 'competent person' with health and safety responsibilities usually one of the owners in smaller firms, or a member of staff trained in health and safety.

You'll normally be responsible for:
- Fire safety.
- Safety of electrical equipment.
- Gas safety - maintaining equipment, including annual inspections.
- Managing asbestos.

You're also responsible for providing:
- A reasonable temperature.
- Enough space, ventilation and lighting.
- Toilets and washing facilities.
- Drinking water.
- Safety and first aid equipment.

The Health and Safety Executive's **'Workplace health, safety and welfare: a short guide'** has more details and their guidelines show how you can assess the risks in your workplace.

Step 1 - Identify the hazards.
Step 2 - Decide who might be harmed and how.
Step 3 - Evaluate the risks and decide on precautions.
Step 4 - Record your findings and implement them.
Step 5 - Review your assessment and update if necessary.

The Health and Safety Executive (HSE) and local councils are responsible for making sure you follow the law. You can access more information of the Health and Safety Executive's website: www.hse.gov.uk

Chapter 10

Trading standards

The Chartered Trading Standards Institute (CTSI) at: www.tradingstandards.uk gives information relating to the sale of goods. The CTSI has taken over ownership of Business Education from the Office of Fair Trading.

The CTSI gives business guidance on compliance with trading standards legislation relating to a range of topics from keeping animals to labelling of foods and selling fireworks. You will also find guidance through your county council trading standards website.

The Sale of Goods Act 1979 (and other legislation) covers a wide range of retailers and goods. It gives your customers certain legal rights when they buy goods from you. As a responsible retailer, you need to know how the Act affects you and your customers - so that your customers stay happy and you stay on the right side of the law.

Consumers have rights and traders must fulfil certain obligations towards consumers. Contracts that involve credit or finance in any form are subject to additional rules. Traders must be aware of what is expected of them.

The Contract of a Sale

When a consumer buys goods and/or services from a trader, both consumer and trader are seen to be entering into a contract. A contract may be defined as an agreement between two or more parties that is intended to be legally binding. The contract may include various express terms and implied terms. Express terms are those that are specifically agreed between both parties - for example, the price in most contracts or an agreed delivery date. Implied terms are those which are deemed to exist even if they have not been specifically agreed - they cover issues such as quality, description and fitness for purpose.

Failure to comply with the terms of the contract is referred to as a breach of contract, and the person committing the breach normally has to correct it in some way. Terms given to a consumer after the contract is made (for example, terms written only on the back of a receipt) are not part of the contract and they have no effect.

A contract does not have to be written down, but where there are key express terms it is advisable to detail these in writing so there can be no dispute later on.

When a trader displays or advertises goods or services (for example, by displaying goods on a shelf in a shop alongside a price ticket) they are giving consumers what is referred to as an 'invitation to treat'. The consumer can then make an offer to buy the goods or services. At this point the trader is under no obligation to accept the offer - a contract is made if and when the trader accepts.

Sometimes, the process works the other way round - that is, the trader makes an offer to the consumer, and a contract is made when the consumer accepts the offer.

Under the contract, the consumer will agree to pay the trader a sum of money and/or do something else, in return for the goods or services the trader supplies. This commitment is known as the 'consideration' in the contract. If there is no consideration (that is, if a trader offers to supply goods or services completely free of any charge or other obligation) there is no contract at all.

The 'implied terms' of a contract

The law provides that in every transaction for the sale and supply of goods, certain terms are implied.

The person transferring or selling the goods must have the right to do so and the goods must:

- **Correspond with the description**: the goods must be 'as described'. If the description is false, a criminal offence may have been committed.
- **Be of a satisfactory quality**: quality is a general term which covers appearance and finish, freedom from minor defects, safety and durability. In assessing quality, price and description must be considered.
- **Be fit for the purpose**: When a consumer indicates that goods are required for a particular purpose or where it is obvious that goods are intended for a particular purpose, and a trader supplies them to meet that requirement, the goods should be fit for that specified purpose.

When the consumer changes their mind

Normally a consumer has no automatic right to change their mind or to cancel a contract. Therefore if this happens they are in breach of contract. Some contracts, for distance selling or selling in a consumers home will allow a period of time for consideration when the consumer does have the option to cancel the contract.

When the consumer cancels the contract wrongfully, the trader may not be able to recover the lost sale and could be entitled to claim loss of profit and any other reasonable costs incurred.

Solutions for breach of contract

When a consumer rejects goods, they can claim compensation for their losses. This will normally amount to a full refund, plus compensation for any foreseeable losses that have been incurred. These losses might include the cost of any property damage caused by the goods, compensation for personal injury and compensation for the additional cost of buying equivalent goods if they are more expensive elsewhere.

The consumer is also released from all their outstanding obligations under the contract - for example, the outstanding instalments in a

contract of hire-purchase. The consumer may be able to demand any of the following in the case of a product defect:
- A repair or replacement.
- A price reduction to an appropriate amount taking the defect into account.
- Return of the goods, part or full refund, and compensation. This amounts to rescission, which is the mutual agreement between the trader and consumer to terminate the contract and restore the position prior to the contract.

Where a consumer demands a repair or replacement, but that remedy would be disproportionate, then the trader would be entitled to offer them one of the other remedies.

Contracts exceptions

- A consumer has no rights in respect of defects that are brought to their attention before the sale, or if the consumer examines the goods before purchase and any defects should have been obvious.
- A consumer cannot claim for damage they cause or if they simply change their mind about wanting the goods.
- A consumer cannot claim if they choose the product themselves for a purpose which is neither obvious nor made known to the trader and they then find that the item is simply unsuitable for that purpose.
- A consumer has no rights to claim for faults that appear as a result of fair wear and tear.

Supply of services

Any service you provide must be carried out:
- With reasonable skill and care.
- For a reasonable price (unless a price has been agreed).
- Within a reasonable time (unless time is an express term - in other words when a completion date has been agreed at the time the contract was made).

Loss or damage in transit

If the trader arranges for goods to be delivered to a consumer, the goods remain at the trader's risk until delivery. Therefore it is the trader's responsibility to ensure that goods are not lost or damaged in transit and/or to take out appropriate insurance.

Misrepresentation

A misrepresentation is a false statement of fact made by a person or their agent that induces someone else to make a contract with them. Dependent upon whether the misrepresentation was made fraudulently, negligently or innocently, the party who has relied on the misrepresentation will be entitled to a remedy that may include rescission, refund and/or compensation.

Unfair Contract Terms Act 1977

This legislation restricts a trader's ability to use contract terms to limit their legal and contractual liabilities. A trader cannot limit or exclude liability for death or personal injury arising from his/her negligence.

In consumer contracts, traders cannot limit or exclude liability for breaches of the implied terms as to description, quality and fitness for purpose of goods. The Chartered Trading Standards Institute at www.tradingstandards.uk gives information on consumer protection from unfair or misleading trading regulations.

The trader's identity

The consumer needs to know or to be able to find out who they are dealing with. A trader's identity and address must be displayed at their place of business, on key business documents and on websites. This information must also be made available to consumers before a contract is made and whenever a consumer requests it.

If a trader fails to disclose that it is a limited company and there is then a breach of contract, the consumer may be able to claim against the directors of the business as individuals. If a trader fails to disclose that it is acting as an agent for someone else, then the consumer may be able to make a claim directly against that trader.

Uncollected goods

Occasionally, consumers fail to collect their goods after having them repaired or forget to pick up ordered goods. It is sufficient to have given notice or have a notice, which is easily visible to consumers, stating how long the trader will keep goods after the agreed date and an intention to dispose of them after this date. The time period would need to be reasonable.

If no notice is given or displayed, the trader may need to send a registered letter to the consumer specifying that the goods are ready for collection and from where. The letter should also state any amount owing. Additional notification must also be given if the trader intends to sell or dispose of the goods after a certain date .

If a consumer states a specific date for delivery of goods and the trader fails to deliver them on time, the consumer has the right to cancel the contract. If the consumer has made 'time of the essence' and the trader has failed to comply, the consumer can treat this as breach of contract and cancel the contract.

It is illegal for a trader to exclude a consumer's statutory rights by, for example, putting a notice in their shop stating that refunds are not given in any circumstances. This is not permitted by law.

Chapter 11

Data Protection and Copyright

Data Protection

Any business, whatever the size is responsible for compliance with customer data security and privacy laws. If you do not comply, you may face fines and/or legal action.

You should be concerned about security and privacy because customer data is a key currency of today's information-based economy. Regardless of the industry you are in, you will probably collect, store, and share customer and employee information. This data may include addresses, email addresses, telephone numbers and credit card/bank account details.

Small businesses are more at risk than large businesses. Data thieves are flexible, they operate using both high and low-tech methods. Small businesses are a particularly attractive target because they often may not have strong data security protection as larger businesses may have.

Compliance is not a choice. You are legally required to comply with the Data Protection Act of 1998 when handling information about clients, employees, or suppliers.

As a small business owner or manager, it is your responsibility to stay current on privacy and security laws affecting your customers, so establish good security and privacy practices from the start.

Protecting copyright

You will find thousands of images of character cakes online. These cakes are either made with the required copyright release which may have cost thousands of pounds, made for display and promotional purposes only, or made without the copyright owners consent and therefore, illegally. Though the risk might seem very small, if you got sued, the legal fees would probably put you out of business. It is wise to state that your business is unable to make cakes using licensed characters unless a written copyright release has been received from the copyright owner.

Copyright law includes cakes made using shaped pans, shaped and carved cakes, and cakes with the image of a licensed character on them. Copyright character tins may only be used by private individuals, for example, when a family makes a cake for a child's birthday party where no sale is involved. Licensed products are for domestic use only. To sell a cake made using a copyrighted character pan would infringe on the cake pan copyright owner's rights.

There is an increasing demand for the use of edible images and tools, like embossers. These images may be copyrighted and some tools enable the production of copyrighted logos and images. The purchase of these items does not allow a business to use an edible copyrighted image, or tools to create a copyrighted image on cakes created for sale. They are designed for personal use only. You can only sell cakes with copyrighted edible images or copyrighted tooled images, if you fulfil the necessary licensing requirements which may incur significant additional cost.

It is a violation of copyright law for a cake decorator to decorate any product they sell with an identical copy or close likeness of copyrighted movie, TV, cartoon, or comic book character without permission of the copyright owners. Therefore, if for example, you created Snow White with a pink dress instead of yellow, you would still be in breach of copyright, unless the copyright and trademark owner authorised your specific use.

The Copyright Act protects against "derivative works" that use copyrighted work as a starting point when creating a new design. Changing Snow White's dress colour would still mean starting with Disney's work, and therefore be an infringement of their copyright. It is possible that it's creation could confuse consumers into thinking that a cake displaying a modified image had actually come from Disney or was authorised by them.

A license may be obtained from the copyright owner to allow the legal use of an image. The same applies to logo artwork, which is also protected by copyright.

As an individual making cakes privately at home for your own family and friends where absolutely no money changes hands (not even to cover expenses), you can do whatever you want. But the law does apply to any bakery trying to make a profit from making and decorating cakes and any private individual who accepts any amount of money for their creations.

If you want to make character cakes for sale, you would have to obtain the necessary licences. Potential fines for copyright violation can run to hundreds of thousands of pounds. It does not matter if you are a private baker working out of your home part time or a large commercial bakery, if you violate the law, you are vulnerable.

The Law - copyright and intellectual property

Copyright law gives the creators of artistic, literary, musical, and other original works, rights to control the ways in which their material may be used. The rights cover public performance or display, copying, adapting, renting or hiring out, and lending copies of the original to the public. It also gives the copyright holder the right to be credited for the work, and to determine who may adapt the work, who may financially benefit from it, and other related rights.

Creating any type of image for commercial purposes, that looks like a copyrighted character is prohibited unless specifically licensed.

However it is worth noting that copyright law recognises two exceptions allowing distribution of copyrighted items and material.

First Sale Doctrine allows the selling on of the physical items like cake pans and tools that create copyrighted images.

Fair Use of copyrighted material includes use for the purposes of criticism, comment, news reporting, teaching, scholarship, and research.

First Sale Doctrine

After the first sale of a particular object that embodies a copyrighted work, the copyright owner's rights are exhausted and the copyrighted object is free to flow in the stream of commerce. The doctrine allows for resale of the copyrighted object. It is important to note, that the First Sale Doctrine does not get around the copyright owner's exclusive right to make reproductions or derivative works.

In the cake world, a baker can purchase a cake pan from a copyright owner or authorized distributor, and then sell that same cake pan to another person without violating the copyright owner's exclusive rights.

However, the First Sale Doctrine does not allow a business to purchase a cake pan from a copyright owner or an authorised distributor and then use the pan to create the copyrighted character cake to sell to a third party.

Licensed pans should not be hired out to consumers by stores (unless the necessary licence is obtained) since the licensor is not earning a royalty from the transaction. Further to this, any bakery, private baker or decorator that sells cakes made from these pans is breaking copyright law.

The same principles of First Sale Doctrine apply to edible images and tools, like embossers, carrying logos and other copyright images. The item itself can be sold on, but purchase of the item does not authorise it's use commercially, on cakes for sale.

Fair use

Fair Use allows use of copyrighted materials without obtaining permission as long as the use can be considered fair. Each use is analysed to determine whether the use is fair regarding:

- Purpose and character.
- The nature of the work.
- The amount of the original work being used.
- The market effect, or how the use impacts the market for the original work.

The goal is to achieve a balance between the rights of the copyright holder and the rights of the public. Fair use can be applied to any medium. When applying the Fair Use Doctrine to cake businesses, a cake baker who uses a character pan to create a character cake cannot hide behind the Fair Use Doctrine to sell the cake, because the purpose of the cake sale is profit.

In a bakery, the ultimate use is for profit, theoretically at least! But you could argue that the use of a copyright image on a cake for a private birthday party has no major impact on the general market for the artwork. Some customers may purchase figures and bring them to a cake decorator to use, but many will just find someone else willing to break the law so they can have a cake with the decorations they want. The dilemma remains but so does the risk.

If you want to create cakes with licensed characters you have two legal options:

- Contact the copyright owners to obtain, in writing, a release for each one time use. This may take some time and can be very expensive.
- The customer may purchase a license for and individual character cake design, for you to create the cake.
- Purchase licensed figures. Many cake decorators stock a range of pre-made character figurines, like Mickey Mouse and Spongebob for example, for use on cakes. These can be sold to customers so that they can use them on their cakes.

If you wish to repeatedly use the same character, logo or artwork, you might be able to negotiate a blanket license from the copyright holder. So if you wanted to put a particular copyrighted character on many cakes, you might be able to negotiate a license for multiple use. It is entirely up to the copyright holder, so every case is different. Remember that if you make cakes for your business and you and/or your customers take pictures of the cakes for promotion or just to keep, those pictures make for permanent evidence of any legal or illegal use of copyrighted material as long as that photo exists online, in print, in portfolios or albums.

Your copyright

Copyright law works in the same way to protect your own rights as a creator of original artwork. It is an automatic right that arises whenever an individual or a company creates a work. To qualify, the piece of work, (which may be your original cake creation, or a drawing of your unique design), it should be regarded as original, and exhibit a degree of labour, skill or judgement.

Copyright applies to an independent, actual creation rather than the idea behind that creation. Your idea for a cake design is not in itself protected, but the actual completed cake that you create would be. Names, titles, short phrases and colours are not unique or significant enough to be covered, but a logo or particular image that combines these elements might be.

The individual, or group of individuals who create a work automatically own the work and the copyright. They are referred to as the 'first owner of copyright' under the 1988 Copyright, Designs and Patents Act. However, if a work is produced as part of employment then the first owner is usually the company that employs the individual who created the work. So if you employ somebody to create original cake designs, you will own the copyright.

Freelance or commissioned work usually belongs to the author of the work, unless there is an agreement stating otherwise, for example, a contract for service indicating that the copyright ownership will be with the person or organisation commissioning the work. Copyright on anything, may be transferred or sold by the copyright owner to another party.

Your ideas cannot be copyrighted. In the case of business ideas or individual's ideas, it is only the recorded work rather than an intangible idea that is protected. Copyright would apply to items such as written documents, artwork, etc. for example: an illustration, business plan, promotional poster, website, logo, and items can certainly be registered. If a competitor used your work by copying or adapting your poster or a logo, or stole content from your website to promote their business or product, you could certainly take action, as this would be a breach of copyright.

There is very little you can do to prevent someone else starting a business based on a similar idea. If they do not directly copy your work or poach customers by passing off, this is regarded as fair competition.

Duration of copyright

The Copyright, Designs and Patents Act of 1988 states that the duration of copyright is 70 years from the end of the year in which the last author of the work dies. This is the case for literary, artistic and musical works.

Protecting copyright

Copyright notices help to reduce risk of misuse and to maintain your copyright ownership. The notice should be obvious and legible, and whenever possible, the notice should appear on every page. Mark your work with the notice, on the body of the work as well as the cover or sleeve.
- The notice should include the actual term copyright. The notice should include the copyright symbol © and the year.
- The notice should also state when it was first published, or for unpublished work, the year it was created.
- The notice should include name of the owner - an individual, collective or an organisation, for example - Copyright © 2016 The Cake Makery.

Additional evidence of your copyright ownership can help in case of dispute. This may include:
- A footprint within software (deliberate mistakes, algorithms etc.)

which can identify you as the author.
- Watermarks or messages/titles within electronic images.
- Keep as much of the background work as you can, working plans, rough sketches and draft versions etc.

Registering your work

Copyright ownership is automatic but registering that copyright is voluntary. The evidence that registration provides may be particularly important if the work has high commercial value, and it is recommended in such cases.

You may wish to register a logo which would appear on all images of your cakes. This would be more practical than registering individual cake designs. Include the copyright mark, date and your name wherever you can on design work and images.

If you do wish to register logos or images you can find details on The UK Copyright Service website: www.copyrightservice.co.uk. This would give you independent evidence to substantiate your claim in case of a dispute. Once registered, you are also permitted to state: "This work is registered with the UK Copyright Service" as an extra deterrent against infringement.

Only the owner of the work, or his exclusive licensee can bring proceedings in court against an infringement.

Trademarks and logos

A trademark is a sign which can distinguish your goods and services from those of your competitors. Your trademark is your "brand". It can be name, words, slogan, design, symbol, or other unique device or a combination, that identifies a product or organisation. You can use your trademark in your marketing so that customers can recognise your products and services. The only way to register your trademark is to apply to The Intellectual Property Office (IPO).

You cannot make any changes to your trademark after it has been registered so you will need to think carefully about the nature of your trademark before taking the decision to register.

There is a non-refundable application fee although this does not guarantee registration of your trademark. The cost can increase considerably if you require trademark registration in more than one class or if you are registering a logo rather than plain text. Classes are areas of trade and are complicated to understand. It is therefore advisable to submit an application to register a trademark via a professional service.

To proceed with registration you will need:
- Details for your trademark, e.g. an illustration or words/slogan.
- The trademark classes you want to register for.

Trademarks will be acceptable if they are distinctive. They need to be able to be recognised as signs that differentiate your goods or service from someone else's. They are not there to describe the goods or services but they need to be identifiable to be a registrable trademark. If you are confident that your trademark is acceptable, you can apply to register it online. A registered trademark must be renewed every ten years to keep it in force.

A trademark is not registrable if it:
- Describes your goods or services in any way.
- Has become common in your line of work.
- Is not distinctive.
- Is three dimensional or if the shape is typical of the goods or part of, the goods you are involved with.
- Has a function or adds value to your goods.
- Includes specially protected emblems.
- Is offensive.
- Is against the law, e.g. promoting illegal drugs.
- Is deceptive.

Details of how to apply and examples of acceptable and unacceptable trademarks are available on the IPO's website.

If your trademark meets the criteria for registration it will be published in the Trade Marks Journal. This allows third parties the opportunity to object to the application. If there is no opposition following the publication period, your trademark will be registered.

It usually takes about 3 months to register a trademark if no objec-
tions are raised.

Logos
A logo is a graphical element, a symbol, emblem, or sign, that
together with its logotype (which may be a unique set or arrangement
of type), can form a trademark or commercial brand. Typically, a
logo design is for quick recognition, inspiring loyalty, trust and an
implied superiority. A logo is a part of a company's commercial
brand. It's shape, colours, fonts, and images usually stand out as
different from others of similar businesses. Logos can also be used to
identify numerous other organisations and non-commercial entities.

Your logo can form part of your trademark. You do not have to, but
the only way to truly protect your trademark, is to register it by
applying to the IPO.

Chapter 12

Dealing with Customers and Orders

Time Management

Time management is considered necessary because you cannot store time. Available time is limited and if unused, it is lost forever. Most people and businesses have more than one goal and they will sometimes conflict, not all goals are of equal priority, and may not be able to be accomplished without the application of effort, which requires the use of time.

Time management is used to increase effectiveness, efficiency and/or productivity. It is the process of planning and exercising control over the amount of time spent on specific tasks or activities. Time management tools and techniques may be used to manage time when accomplishing specific tasks, projects and/or goals within particular time scales and delivery times. A good time management system is regarded as essential in any business.

Becoming a cake decorator requires more than simply icing and decorating cakes, creating edible flowers or modelling animals and figures. The responsibilities of the job range from financial to creative duties. It will involve planning, control and overall management of several projects at a time.

Although working as a cake decorator may be stressful at times, it is important to remember the rewarding aspects - you will be satisfying your customers by delivering amazing, individually customised creations.

Many cake businesses will produce a set range of designs or types of cake. It must be your decision whether each of your creations is an original piece of work or if you choose to produce a set range of designs that individuals can choose from. You may be choosing between charging significantly more for individually created designs or a range of cheaper priced goods in larger numbers. This will affect the way you work. Do you prefer working on one detailed piece or on a bulk order of many similar cakes?

With multiple orders and customers, completing cakes for specific deadlines and for particular special events can be stressful and at times it may seem overwhelming. You need to be able to manage time properly when working on several different cake projects.

Working with a schedule to time manage all the cakes you have on order at any one time is vital. It will enable you to fulfil orders in an organised time-frame giving you the necessary time to complete the design and decoration process without feeling rushed and under unnecessary pressure.

Remember that you also need time to complete all your business paperwork. Accounting, bookkeeping, processing orders, making phone calls to clients, venues, suppliers etc., and ordering ingredients and products all need to be part of your time management process.

If you never have enough time to finish your tasks, better time management will help you regain control of your day making your business more efficient and profitable. Good time management does not mean you do more work, but helps you to focus on the tasks that matter. Learning how to manage your time effectively will help you feel more relaxed, focused and in control.

Improve your time management by working out what you want your business to achieve and what your priorities are for the business. This will give you some guiding principles for how your time is best used for the benefit of your business and how you manage it. If you have

165

an idea of the bigger picture, however general, you can then work out short-term and medium-term goals. This will help you plan better and focus on the things that will help you achieve those goals.

A common time management mistake is trying to remember too many details, leading to information overload. Stay organised and take control of your projects and tasks by using a to-do list to write things down. Then you can deal with one task at a time, putting your whole energy to the task in hand whilst knowing that your time plan will ensure you complete all the required jobs on your to-do list.

Find out what works best for you. You may prefer to keep a single to-do list, to avoid losing track of multiple orders and tasks. Keeping a list will help you work out your priorities and timings, it can help you put off the non-urgent tasks. You may develop a more comprehensive time management plan to organise individual tasks and orders as the business grows.

Good time management enables high-quality work, not quantity. Many people work through without breaks to gain extra time at work, but this can be counter-productive. As a general rule, taking regular breaks away from your work will help you to be more effective, focussed and productive when you come back to it.

Schedule for time management
You will probably find it helpful to check what you have ahead for that day first thing in the morning, and always finish the day having prepared for the next day. You may like to use daily to-do plans to help you identify a few items listed to complete on that day, with the reason for doing them and a timeline for getting them done.

Long term planner
Use a daily, weekly or even monthly planner to write down appoint-ments, orders, and meetings in a chronological order. This could be in the form of a log book or chart. Use a monthly chart so that you can plan further ahead. Long term planners will also serve as a reminder to constructively plan time for yourself and to set long term goals for your business.

Taking an Enquiry - Where to Start?

When you are approached with a request for a cake, be it for family, a friend or a paying customer, take time to consider the elements before committing to the cake.

Upon receiving the initial enquiry, take some basic information: date, type/size of cake, and the occasion. If you have a very busy order book, it may be wise to take a few moments to go away and check this (giving yourself the time to think and consider rationally) before a quick call back to confirm your availability.

Once you are committed to an enquiry, there are a few questions that you will want answered.

This list will identify the important questions you need to asks:
- What is the date and time of the event?
- Does the customer have a budget?
- How many guests will the cake need to serve?
- Is it to be served as a dessert alternative (this may alter the cut size of portions and therefore the quantity of cake required)?
- What flavours and fillings are required?
- Are there any special dietary requirements?
- What shape and number of tiers (if applicable) is preferred?
- Is a cutting cake (sometimes called a 'kitchen cake') required?
- Is a fruit cake required to be kept, uncut?
- Does the customer have any ideas of her own regarding style, colour, design for the cake?
- What and where is the venue
- Is delivery and set-up required?
- Will you charge extra for delivery?
- What time is the event (if there is a different reception venue, when are the guests expected to arrive there) especially important for your time planning if you are delivering other cakes that day.
- Have you been provided with any reference – colours, fabrics, photos, pictures of similar cakes etc., which may help the design process?

When you have started to gather together this information, you will be able to discuss and develop designs with confidence. Being able to convey your ideas with clarity, will give both you and your client confidence that you can deliver a stunning and personal cake, a vital requirement if you aim to develop a successful business.

Make sure, that when designing wedding cakes, you keep those significant details that you have already gathered together, in mind as you progress the order.

Do not forget these less obvious considerations:
- Is the cake going to be too heavy to lift in one piece?
- Will it fit in the car (yours or theirs)?
- Remember to consider the size of the cake once it is boxed – how many boxes will you need?
- Is the time of year, e.g. hot summer weather, going to affect the cake in transit or at the venue?
- Does the venue have a cobbled drive?!
- Is there a long walk between the car and the cake table?
- Will you need help carrying it?
- Where is the cake to be displayed? A small cake may get lost from view if not raised.
- Is the table for the cake in a busy place? Make sure it won't get knocked by guests or staff.
- If it is a marquee reception, will heat (or moisture on a wet day) affect the cake, and is the floor level?
- Is it practical to finish off last minute details at the venue?
- When do you expect to be paid and do you require a deposit (always a good idea)?

This list is not intended to put you off, but is designed to keep you prepared and enable you to avoid potential pitfalls. This will give you confidence throughout the whole process.

Preparation is everything

- Confirm the order details, as you understand them, in writing, to your customer before progressing with the cake.
- Order well in advance any additional items like boxes, boards, ribbons and stands etc.

- Contact the florist if relevant for the cakes completion. If necessary, agree a time to set up when the florist is there or has delivered the flowers.
- Always contact the venue well before the event to plan the best delivery and set-up time.
- Plan your journey and the timing carefully so that you do not arrive in a fluster.
- Allow time and flexibility for heavy traffic, or for a venue which is not prepared and ready for your arrival.
- Be prepared – take an emergency kit when setting up your cakes.

Keeping records of orders

Make sure you keep all the necessary contact details for your customer together. Include agreed costs, deposit paid, event time (and, if necessary, expected arrival time at the venue), florist details, catering contacts and venue details.

You may have been supplied with additional items: models or reference material e.g. photographs. Make sure you keep these together with the customer details, or note carefully where you have stored items. If you have been given items or models for a cake that are bulkier, make sure you note where they are stored so that you can still find them easily, several months later when they are required for the cake.

Keep records of your meetings, details of your customer's requirements and any modifications together with all other details for that customer. This will give you all you need, in one place, enabling you to plan the schedule for cooking, icing and decoration as well as, order items and ingredients in advance. If you beginning to build your business, this time planning will be invaluable when you are planning and juggling a growing number of cake orders.

Useful Forms

This section will take you through many forms that have proved invaluable for me in my business, and which I hope you will find useful.

We have included samples of all the forms, which you can use as a basis for creating your own business forms. Add your own business name, address and contact details as well as your logo if desired. If you have a stationery style established for letterheads and business cards then this style can be applied to these forms as well.

Spending a bit of time putting together some smart looking forms will ensure you come across as a well organised and professional looking business.

Although many high street printers will be able to create these for you at a reasonable cost, the forms can be quite easily created yourself on your own computer and there are many templates within programmes like Word for Windows or Mac, and Pages for Mac, that will help you create them. This incurs little or no cost except for that of printing them out as required.

Telephone enquiry form

The first contact you will have with many potential customers, will often be via a phone conversation. However, it may not be you taking the call. If yours is a home based business, another member of your household might answer the phone.

For this reason, it is a good idea to establish, within your household, how the phone will be answered and, if necessary, a few rules about who can answer the phone. A first impression given by your ten-year-old saying 'Hello!' may not quite be the professional impression you intended!

It is also very useful to provide a prompt sheet to aid whoever answers the phone. This will ensure they can gather some essential and useful information to aid you when you have the opportunity to follow up the enquiry.

Telephone Enquiry Form

Date: _____ Name: _____ Source:_____
Address:_____
_____ Postcode: _____
Tel: Day :_____ Eve:_____ Mob:_____
Date required: _____ Occasion: _____
Summary:

_____

Date: _____ Name: _____ Source:_____
Address:_____
_____ Postcode: _____
Tel: Day :_____ Eve:_____ Mob:_____
Date required: _____ Occasion: _____
Summary:

_____

Date: _____ Name: _____ Source:_____
Address:_____
_____ Postcode: _____
Tel: Day :_____ Eve:_____ Mob:_____
Date required: _____ Occasion: _____
Summary:

_____

Date: _____ Name: _____ Source:_____
Address:_____
_____ Postcode: _____
Tel: Day :_____ Eve:_____ Mob:_____
Date required: _____ Occasion: _____
Summary:

Confirmation of Order and Terms and Conditions

The first, and one of the most useful, forms you will need is a confirmation of the basic details of an order with your customer once it has been received.

This form will state clearly to your customer, all that you have agreed. You can outline a brief description of the order and include other details as you feel appropriate.

The example here includes all the necessary contact details of your customer, the date the order was taken and the date for which the cake is required.

Further to this, it includes some basic information about the cake. You can include details of additional items like hired stands or whether flowers are being supplied by the florist or yourself.

Include any financial arrangements. It is important to include details of any deposit paid, balance and due date as well as any delivery and/or hire charges as appropriate.

It is entirely up to you, how much detail you choose to include. This form does not set out all the details in stone, but will ensure that if changes are made, everyone is starting with the same information.

You must ensure you have all this information retained for your own purposes to refer to, modify, and add to as necessary whilst fulfilling the order. This form need not be duplicated. It is handed to your customer upon receipt of their deposit.

It is a good idea to keep a job sheet (example in the next pages) for every order inside a plastic sleeve, allowing you to keep additional information, ribbon & fabric samples, and photographs, etc. all in one place. If you have additional items, e.g. a cake topper, make a note on your job sheet, of where it is stored. This will not only remind you where it is but also, that you already have it!

Confirmation of Order

Order date: _____ Required date: _____ Time: _____

Occasion: _____

Name: _____

Address: _____

_____

Tel no: _____ Mobile: _____ Email: _____

Delivery address (if applicable): _____

_____

_____ Tel no: _____

Cake type(s), fillings, size, shape & number of tiers:

_____

Cutting cake (if applicable): _____ Number of portions: _____

Type of icing: _____ Base colour: _____

Design and decoration summary:

Pillars/Stand requirement: _____

Cake stand required? _____ Knife (and spray?) required?_____

Flower requirements?

Cake price: _____ £ . . . .

Delivery charges: (if applicable): _____ £ . . . .

Hire charges (if applicable): _____ £ . . . .

TOTAL COST: _____ £ _____

Less deposit received: _____ £ . . . .

BALANCE: _____ Due on or before: _____ £ _____

No VAT is chargeable

Please see reverse for Terms and Conditions

COMPANY NAME AND ADDRESS

173

Terms and Conditions

We would recommend printing your Terms and Conditions onto the reverse of the Confirmation of Order so that your customer has all the order details and your terms and conditions together.

Spend some time to consider your Terms and Conditions carefully. Ensure that they meet your particular business needs. Study other business's terms and conditions to help you build your own which include exactly what you need.

Consider including terms and conditions for payments, cancellations, equipment hire, modifications or alterations. Include details about what will happen if an event date, or venue changes.

Everyone is different, but you should consider copyright and design ownership issues carefully. Explain your position upon reproducing copyrighted material and include also, how your copyright works.

You may also wish to state terms on who is responsible for a cake when an order is delivered or collected from your premises.

The terms and conditions included here are designed as a prompt for you to use to generate your own, covering all your particular needs.

Our example gives quite an extensive set of inclusions. You may select just those terms that suit you from this list, or add more terms that you feel suit your particular business. The underlined blank areas are where your business name will appear.

Terms and Conditions

Payments

In the unlikely event that you have problems with your event arrangements, which may include payments for services from _____, it is recommended that you take out insurance to cover all eventualities. This will give both you and your party service providers 'peace of mind' and will avoid any unnecessary problems. Payments to _____ can be made in cash, by BACs to account no: _____ sort code: _____ or by cheques payable to _____ .

Deposits

All cakes require a non-refundable deposit of 20% of the total cost which will become due once the order has been placed and details checked and agreed by you. The balance becomes due 28 days before the date of the Event. Please note, that if full payment of the cake is not received by the date requested, it is assumed that the cake has been cancelled unless you are paying by prior arrangement, upon collection, your cake will not be delivered.

Cancellation Policy

If for any reason it is necessary for you to cancel your cake order, work already completed is chargeable. If you cancel your cake order after full payment has been made, no refunds will be made to you (the client) under any circumstances. We recommend that you take out wedding insurance to cover all possible eventualities.

Equipment Hire

All equipment requires a deposit. The deposit will be reimbursed in full to the hirer on safe return of the hired equipment provided it has not suffered any damage whatsoever. Damage includes: cuts, chips, scratches, breakages, cracks, rips, tears, dents, bending, staining and discolouration. All hired equipment should be clean and in the original packaging provided. Violation of any signed agreements can result in _____ withholding the deposit in part or full. In addition, late return of the hired equipment may carry further penalty up to the value of the deposit.

Alterations to Orders

Any alterations to the original order must be confirmed in writing and may be subject to an additional charge. Late amendments to orders are often possible and every effort will be made to accommodate changes, but this cannot be guaranteed and may incur additional charges.

Change of Event Date

If, for any reason you wish to re-arrange the date of your event, _____ will try its best to accommodate these changes without any additional charges provided sufficient notice is given and that we are able to provide a cake for the re-arranged event date. However, if we are fully booked on your new event date and cannot provide the event cake, it will not be possible to refund your 20% deposit. The limiting factor with any cake provision is usually the cake set-up. As a compromise, it may be possible to provide you with a cake prior to your event date, but under these circumstances it will become your responsibility to collect, deliver and set-up the cake at the venue. If you cancel your cake order with _____ after requesting a change of date no refunds will be made to you (the client) under any circumstances. We recommend that you take out insurance to cover all eventualities.

Setting-Up

Whilst _____ will try to ensure that your cake is presented at its very best we cannot be held responsible for the location of the cake at the venue, the stability or levelness of the surface where the cake is displayed or the quality of the area surrounding the cake. Please ensure, therefore, that the surface or table for the cake is level, stable and strong enough to hold the cake. A five tier rich fruit wedding cake could easily weight up to 7Kg. Please also remember that chocolate covered and filled cakes can melt under extreme conditions as you may experience within a marquee on a hot summers day. Once the cake has been collected or delivered, set-up, and signed for _____ cannot be held responsible for any interference or damage to the cake.

176

Colourings and Ingredients

_____ does not guarantee to match exact colours and designs chosen due to the fact that our cakes are handmade by us in our kitchens and may vary despite every effort being made. We also cannot guarantee that all the product-lines used in the cakes will be available at the time of making. For example, when a supplier de-lists an item such as a pre-made flower spray or a particular ribbon colour we will endeavour to re-design a cake to reflect as closely as possible the original design using alternative products. Please be aware that whilst your chosen cake may be made without nuts or nut products, it will be prepared in a kitchen where nut products may be used in other cakes and fillings. _____ recommend that sugarpaste items on your cake with a high concentrate of colouring, are not eaten. The decorations may also contain wires, jewels and other non-edible products, these will be noted in our disclaimer for each cake supplied. It is yours or your caterer's responsibility to ensure that these non-edible products are removed before serving the cake to yourself or your guests. Alternatively, we can provide a fully edible cake that is not so highly decorated or coloured.

Publication and Promotional Rights.

By signing the Order Form the client agrees that _____ is the sole designer and owner of the final cake design. All cake designs remain the property of _____. The client has no ownership rights over any cake design. We reserve the right to re-use and publish our photographs of the client's cake as and when required. Whilst we try to ensure that all published designs are exclusive to _____, we do not guaranteed exclusivity of cake designs between our clients.

Ownership Rights

The relationship between the client and _____ and the ownership of the product(s) purchased by the client from _____ are clear in law. The client owns the cake once delivered to the venue or collected from _____. If the client fails to pay the full amount for the cake and/or products, as agreed and stated on the order form, then ownership of the products remains with _____ _____ and not the client. The responsibility of ensuring the cake remains in good order lies with the owner of the cake. The transfer of ownership also equates to the transfer of responsibility. It becomes the client's responsibility to ensure the cake remains in good order when ownership of the cake is transferred to the client.

Design Rights

The ownership of the cake design remains with _____ and is not transferred on ownership of the product to the client. This is important because it means that _____ has the right to publish and sell the design to other clients. During the consultation process the client views a range of existing cake designs developed exclusively by _____.
The client selects a design, part or combinations of various designs developed by the company. This is standard practice within the industry.

Unique Designs

Whilst an individual cake design is not exclusive to the client the cake design will be exclusive to _____. In addition, since all cakes are hand-made and not mass-produced every cake is different. The chances of another client requesting exactly the same cake design is very small, so it is likely that your cake design will be exclusive to you, however this is not guaranteed. Minor changes to our designs, is one way of keeping your cake relatively exclusive. It is unlikely that we will publish a similar cake design twice. This may mean that cakes published in the past and in the future may look similar but not the same as the customers design.

External Published Designs

_____ will not make exact copies of other cake designs produced by other UK registered cake companies. In addition _____ will not make exact copies of other copyrighted designs of any form. This ensures that cakes within the industry remain exclusive to the companies who create them and also ensures that there is a large variety of cake designs available to clients and helps maintain exclusivity. It is also healthy for the industry and avoids infringement of copyright law.

The Design Process

During an initial consultation _____ will discuss and obtain from the client a list of requirements for their cake. Once these requirements are accepted and the basis of a design agreed with the client an order confirmation is written out and agreed, listing these requirements. A deposit is paid by the client. The deposit pays for the ingredients, an initial design idea and the reservation date. _____ will finalise any design details and draw up the agreed design to meet those requirements.

Note: This appears here as a very lengthy list, but once reduced to 'small print' this fits on the reverse of an A4 Confirmation of Order.

Invoices and Receipts

It is very important that you keep on top of your paperwork. Maintain a system of invoicing jobs promptly to ensure prompt payments from your customers.

Receipting payments will guarantee that it is clear to all parties what is paid and what is not, particularly when you are dealing with deposits, possible instalments and final payments.

Remember that if you are VAT registered, all your company stationery must carry your VAT registration number. You should state clearly the address, date, invoice number, when payment is expected and to whom it should be paid. You can include methods by which payment can be accepted e.g. credit cards, cheques, cash, Paypal and/or BACs.

Make sure that you describe clearly, exactly what the invoice is for and make clear what is included and what is not. State items such as cake stands and knife hire, delivery and set-up costs, so that there is no chance of misunderstanding. Make it clear where additional items like fresh flowers are being used on a cake, whether they will be provided by you (the cake maker) and are therefore part of your invoice, or by the florist and therefore invoiced to the customer directly from the florist?

Always keep a copy of the invoice on file as this provides information for accounting purposes as well as a reference of your dealings with customers.

Receipts are not always required. A simple signature of acceptance on the original invoice may be sufficient to acknowledge receipt of payment. Some customers may require a separate receipt so it is a good idea to have a receipt form available for use as required.

Make sure you keep accurate accounting records of all payments, whether they are deposits, instalments or final payments. Keep records with the customer name, stating clearly the type of payment received, the job number, the date, and the amount paid.

On the following pages are examples of an invoice and a receipt.

Invoice

To:

Invoice Number: _____

Invoice Date: _____

Description: Amount

Sub Total   _____

VAT (if applicable)   _____

Less Deposit Paid   _____

TOTAL   _____

Payment due within 28 days

Please make payment by BACs, cash or cheque payable to: Company name

Include VAT number if applicable

COMPANY NAME, ADDRESS, TELEPHONE

Receipting payments will guarantee that it is clear to all parties what is paid and what is not, particularly when you are dealing with deposits, possible instalments and final payments.

It is wise to have a receipt form although it may not always necessary to provide a physical receipt, an email or signed invoice may suffice. It looks more professional than a scrap of paper if a customer does ask for a receipt!

Receipt	
To:	Receipt Number: _____ Receipt Date: _____

Thank you for your payment received:

Details: _____

_____

Amount received: _____

Signed: _____

COMPANY NAME, ADDRESS, TELEPHONE

Hire forms

You may choose to use an additional form for hiring of equipment if this is something you do quite a lot. This form would need to state the item to be hired, the hire period, charge for the period, deposit if applicable, VAT if applicable and the expected date of return.

Hire Agreement

To:

Agreement Number: _____

Agreement Date: _____

ITEM CODE: _____   ITEM DESCRIPTION: _____

HIRE FROM DATE: _____   ITEM DESCRIPTION: _____

HIRE FEE: _____   PAID DATE: _____

DEPOSIT AMOUNT: _____   PAID DATE: _____

COMPANY NAME, ADDRESS, TELEPHONE

State your terms and conditions of hire on the reverse of the booking form. It is a good idea to retain a record book of hire items so that you can quickly identify items that are available or booked out at any particular time.

Terms and Conditions of Hire

All equipment requires a deposit. The deposit will be reimbursed in full to the hirer on safe return of the hired equipment provided it has not suffered any damage whatsoever.

Damage includes: cuts, chips, scratches, breakages, cracks, rips, tears, dents, bending, staining and discolouration.

All hired equipment should be clean and in the original packaging provided.

Violation of any signed agreements can result in _____ withholding the deposit in part or full.

In addition, late return of the hired equipment may carry further penalty up to the value of the deposit.

Disclaimers, important information forms

This form can be used by yourself to explain any inedible materials used, to indicate cakes of different flavours, and even details like cakes to be retained uncut. Use the form to pass on any information to whomever you are handing the responsibility of the cake to when you deliver. This form should be signed in duplicate, one copy to be retained by the customer (or customers representative), and one to be retained by you.

Sometimes, you may be unable to set up the cake because the venue is not ready for you. It may be wise not to guarantee set-up on this basis. The cake may need to be signed over to someone else who will set it up and take responsibility for it. For this reason it is always wise to use a disclaimer form.

Disclaimer

Important Information

Customer/Supplier copy

Cake(s) supplied to: _____

Please note, for the safety of those eating the cake, I am bringing to your attention the following for which I would appreciate your acknowledgment. These items must be removed before cutting and eating the cake. If you are not cutting the cake yourself, please pass this information on to the person concerned.

Inedible products: _____

_____

_____

Special notes: _____

_____

I acknowledge receipt of the above information. Thank you.

Signed: _____

Print name: _____Date: _____

Cake(s) supplied by: COMPANY NAME, ADDRESS, TELEPHONE

Job sheets

A job sheet for every order is invaluable to keep track of all the details that will become part of an order. Some celebration cake and wedding cake orders will have many elements and stages. For this reason alone it is vitally important you keep track of every detail to ensure that all runs smoothly on the delivery day. Keeping the job sheet in a plastic sleeve is a good way of keeping details together with any correspondence or other reference matter, including a note of items that might be collected for the order, but stored elsewhere. The example job sheets can be modified as required for a general cake order and one for a more detailed wedding cake order.

184

General Cake Job Sheet

DUE DATE - inc DAY/TIME: _____ **JOB NO.** _____

Enquiry received: _____ Ordered: _____

Customer details, Name _____

Address _____

_____ Postcode _____

Tel no _____ Mobile_____ Email _____

Venue for delivery _____

_____Date/time of delivery:_____

Contact name at venue _____ Tel no _____

Catering contact _____ Tel no _____

Florist contact _____ Tel no _____

Price quoted: £_____ Date _____

Deposit paid £_____ Date _____

Changes to quote _____ Date _____

Changes to quote _____ Date _____

Final Payment: £_____ Invoice date _____

Received date _____

Occasion _____

Names/wording to include on cake _____

_____

Kind/shapes/sizes of cake

Number of portions required _____

_____

Design details

Wedding Cake Job Sheet

DUE DATE - inc DAY/TIME: _____ JOB NO. _____

Enquiry received: _____ Ordered: _____

Customer details, name _____

Address _____

_____ Postcode _____

Tel no _____ Mobile_____ Email _____

Venue for delivery _____

_____Date/time of delivery:_____

Contact name at venue _____ Tel no _____

Catering contact _____ Tel no _____

Florist contact _____ Tel no _____

Price quoted: £_____ Date _____

Deposit received: £_____ Date _____

Design sent _____ Approved Date _____

Additions/deductions/modifications _____ Date _____

Additions/deductions/modifications _____ Date _____

Final invoice: £_____ Date _____ Received _____

Colour of bride's dress/flowers _____Sample supplied?   YES/NO

Detail (embroidery, frills etc) flowers in bouquet etc.

_____

Colour of bridesmaid's dresses _____ Sample supplied? YES/NO

Shape of cake(s) and size of each tier_____

Portions required _____ No. of tiers _____ Cutting cake required? _____

Type of cake (fruit or other)

_____

Type of icing preferred _____ Base cake colour _____

Main decoration colour(s) _____

Top ornament or arrangement

_____

Other decoration or ornament ideas

_____

Pillars/Stand requirement _____

Cake stand and knife requirements (knife spray?) _____

Details of display area for cake _____

Notes:

Final Details

Once you have progressed through an order and have finally arrived at the point of delivery or collection, the paperwork is done and the finances dealt with, give yourself enough time for a final check.

Double-check everything before the cake is collected, or before leaving your premises with a cake, to travel to a venue. Double check everything again before leaving a cake at a venue.

Take a photograph of the cake before collection or, at the venue as security. This will confirm that your cake was in good order. Should there be any problems after collection or after you leave the venue, this photograph is evidence of how you presented the cake. Do this even if you are not leaving a cake set up in it's final position. It is a clear record of the state of a cake at the time you handed over responsibility to the third party who signed your disclaimer agreement.

At a venue, check that all tiered or stacked cakes are sitting correctly, centred or lined up as required. Ensure that separators, pillars and stands are straight, ribbons even and that cakes are aligned from all angles.

Make sure removable decorations are secure and in position (with no pieces of foam left from supporting items in transit!).

Do a final check from all angles that the cake may be viewed from and check your photograph **before** leaving. It is often possible to spot something out of place in a photograph, which you had not noticed whilst looking at the actual cake. At this point, you will still be able to return to the cake, and make adjustments if you are not absolutely happy.

Make sure whoever is responsible for serving the cake knows of any inedible items that need to be removed before serving. Use your disclaimer to give details of these if necessary. Ask for two copies to be signed, one for you to keep and one to be retained by the responsible person.

Pricing your Cakes

The section on Pricing Structure in Chapter 2 explains how to calculate a realistic hourly rate with an aim to build a profitable business. That information will ensure you charge appropriately, whilst covering ALL your business costs. Whatever pricing system you develop for your cake business needs to more than cover all your business costs and taxes to allow your business to make a profit.

The following section guides you through the pricing process when providing quotes for your customers. Pricing cakes is particularly difficult, especially if you are starting from scratch. Many people undercharge for their cakes for a long time before gaining the confidence needed to command more reasonable prices. Your cakes will be taken home by customers, destroyed and eaten, so it is very hard to gauge how you should price them.

Try visiting wedding fairs as a customer. Ask for quotes on cakes – maybe a photo of one of yours or just a magazine picture. It will quickly give you indicators as to how your pricing may compare to your competitors, and it's quite fun too!

A set of pre-calculated example prices for a few 'standards', provides a useful aid when quoting prices - a price for a single, a 2-tier and a 3-tier wedding cake for example. These are basic prices that include covering business costs, for iced standards, a 1, 2 or 3 tiered cake with basic finishing on the cake boards and including boxes. A pre-calculated 'standard' novelty cake price may also be useful. These will give you a starting point when quoting cakes for your customers and help to ensure you will be covering your costs. It may be useful to show your customers what this basic price covers with a simple cake photo.

For your own purposes, establish a basic cost price for all your standard cake sizes and flavours. This will help you when calculating any cake. The basic cost will include ingredients costs, cost of cooking (electricity), marzipan, icing, board and box. It will help you in making final customer calculations if you have a costed time element to complete each basic iced cake. To this basic set of prices, you can add whatever is required for each individual order.

For individual orders do not forget to include the costs of all the items you need, to create any hand made and original decorations. These may be individual to each cake and might include modelling paste, flower paste, wires, flower picks, models, ribbons, artificial flowers, pillars, stands etc. Add these additional costs as required and estimate the time it will take to make the decorations and complete the whole cake. These costs are separate, and in addition to your basic cake costs.

A note on sourcing ingredients - where you get your ingredients and other sugarcraft products from, may have a significant impact on your overall costs and therefore profit margin. Make sure you are getting your supplies at the cheapest possible price but still retaining value. Get your suppliers to work for you by using ones that may offer you trade prices, free delivery if at a distance, and who understand your business.

Mail order companies are very useful, but remember that in an emergency it is good to know a local supplier that stocks the products you require for fast delivery or collection if necessary. Check the terms for payment, can you purchase on account? This may make it easier for you to manage paying your suppliers. You will probably use several suppliers, but remember to regularly check their pricing against their competitors. This will ensure you are always getting the best prices. Do not let them take advantage of your reliable custom.

The Cake Makery's Cost-a-Cake-Pro is a very useful App that makes costing cakes for customers very simple. You can quickly access your basic cakes costs, even while you are with your customer, and you can also use the app to add your own less standard elements, like sugar flower sprays, ready-made or hand-made models, dowels, pillars, wired beads, and even your hourly rate, allowing you to process estimated total cake costs very quickly.

When judging the time required to complete an order, make sure you include time for designing, doing drawings, phone calls, writing emails, washing up, icing cakes, dowelling, wiring flowers, sourcing ornaments/separators, packing cakes and delivering them. Charge a pence per mile cost, but remember to add an element for the time taken to travel too, and don't forget the time taken to set up.

An example Wedding Cake

This is a reasonably detailed wedding cake. It has many elements to consider when calculating the price to quote to your customer. Starting with a sketch we can begin to build a list of what is required.

Piped white lace details on ivory icing

5" Chocolate Cake with Buttercream filling

7" Chocolate cake with Buttercream filling

Vignette of initials and fabric wrap

9" dummy cake with snails trail to complete bottom edge

11" Vanilla Sponge cake with Buttercream filling

Gathered Fabric effect over 13" Fruit cake marzipanned and iced ivory

Iced baseboard to match cake

Start with a sketch, which can also be provided to the customer. The sketch lays out the basic details of the order. This will help you work your way through all the individual elements required, filling in the time and costs. Think your way through the whole cake in your head, jotting down the individual process details as you go. Then estimate the amount of time you think each process will take you to complete.

Once you have done this a few times it will become an easier process that ensures you will not undercharge for your time. It will also help you judge how long an order will take you to complete, and therefore help you gauge your capacity for more orders.

Calculations based on design and customers requirements

Elements of time	Direct costs
Consultations, 1hr/£16 **Design and research** - 4.5hrs/£72 **Drafting designs to fit on cakes** - 1hr/£16	**Cakes (ingredients including, icing, cooking time, electricity & fillings):-** 5" chocolate - £7 7" chocolate - £10.50 11" vanilla - £21 13" fruit cake - £56.50
Preparation (mixing times) Sponge cakes, 3 mixes - 2hrs total/£32 Fruit soak mix - .25hr/£4 Fruit cake mix - 1hr/£16 Wrap and store Fruit cake - .25hr/£4	**Cake boards:** 5" - £1 7" - £1 9" - £1.10 11" - £1.30 Double up 2 x 13"drums - £6 12" Sq for kitchen cake - £2
Filling and levelling: 5" - .25hr/£4 7" - .5hr/£8 11" - .5hr/£8 10" kitchen cake - .5hr/£8	**Other consumables:** Royal icing - £1.20 Ribbon - £3 Dowels - £3 9" dummy - £3 Flowerpaste - £6
Icing cakes: 5" - .25hr/£4 7" - .25hr/£4 9" - .25hr/£4 11" - .5hr/£8 13" including the board - .5hr/£8 10" kitchen cake - .5hr/£8	**Boxes:** 5"& 7" in 2x 8"boxes - £2 Dummy, 11" & 13" in 2 x 16"boxes - £4 (heavy duty box costs £18) 12" kitchen cake box - £2
Marzipan fruit cake 13" - .75hr/£12	**Optional sugar flowers** Casablanca lily spray for top tier - £36
Icing details Icing wrap on 7" - 1hr/£16 Drapes on 13" - 1.5hr/£24 Making initials - monogram - 1.5hr/£24	
Dowelling - 1hr/£16	**TOTALS**
Lace piping detail: 5" - 2hr/£32 7" - 1hr/£16 9" - 2hr/£32 11" - 2.5hrs/£40	**TIME:** 28.5 hours total: £456.00 **MATERIALS:** £131.60 **DELIVERY & SET-UP:** £63.00
Ribbons - .25h/£4	optional flower spray: £36.00
Boxing and photography - 1hr/£16	**GRAND TOTAL:** £650.60 without flower spray
DELIVERY & SET-UP Petrol - 50 miles @ 30p per mile - £15 Time - 1hr/£16 Set-up time 2hrs/£32 (complete lace and trails)	with flower spray: £686.60 *VAT is not applicable*

In this example we have assumed an hourly rate of £16 per hour.

A simpler example first birthday cake

This is a much simpler cake order. A child's birthday cake may seem quick and basic, but when you actually start to break down all the processes and requirements, it is possible to see why so many cake decorators undercharge for their efforts.

8" Chocolate cake with white sugarpaste and buttercream filling

Blue check edible ribbon and bow

Birthday greeting on edible plaque

1 candle

An edible footprint cut out - customer wants real footprint from Freddie

11" iced cake board to match cake

The costings for this cake are laid out below. Use the same process to think through every element just as you would a large wedding cake.

Calculations based on design and customers requirements	
Elements of time	**Direct costs**
Consultation, design time - .5hr/£8 **Preparation time including foot!** - 1.5hr/£24 **Level and fill** - .25hr/£4 **Ice cake & board** - .5hr/£8 **Plaque & foot** - .5hr/£8 **Make gingham bow & ribbon** - .5hr/£8	**8" square chocolate cake with buttercream filling** - £16 **Modelling paste** - £5 **Candle** - £1.00 **11" cake drum** - £1.50 **Blue food pen** - £2.50 **11" box** - £1.00

	Cake will be collected	
3.75hrs Time:		**£60.00**
Consumables:		£27.00
GRAND TOTAL:		**£87.00**

Pricing cakes is difficult – cakes are often very detailed and intricate taking hours to complete. Sugarcraft processes are labour-intensive, you might have to spend several days on the details for one wedding cake, and that is inevitably going to be very expensive. But try to remember:

Be realistic:
if that is what it costs, that IS what it costs.

If you become very popular and never seem to be without work, you could rethink your hourly rate. If on the other hand, you find that clients are put off by your hourly rate, then you may need to consider lowering it.

Sometimes it can pay off to accept a lower rate, for example, if you think a client will be a good source of work in future, or if a particular project will give you valuable experience or exposure.

Add all your elements together in appropriate combinations for the individual cake you are designing and explain delivery and set-up costs (pence per mile and a time element for set-up).

You may choose to keep delivery and set-up as a separate cost, giving your customer the option of collection, but do not forget the time it takes to travel and set-up cakes. It is easy to charge for your petrol but your time is just as valuable.

Changes, modifications and adjustments

Explain what will happen if your customer wants to make any changes to the original order. Decide to what extent you are prepared to accept alterations and state a deadline e.g. 28 days, in your terms and conditions. You may be able to consider late changes if they are of less significance, but make your position clear.

There may be times when you make adjustments to the total calculated cost, for example, offering discounts to family or friends. Make sure these customers are aware of the discount they are receiving. You may want to tell them the full price to prevent unwanted callers asking for discounted cakes!

Estimates versus quotes

It is usually advisable to provide an estimate. An estimate is just that, it is your 'guide' to what the particular order will cost. A quote is a fixed price that your customer can hold you to. Think carefully to ensure you are totally happy with a price before providing a quote.

An estimate will allow for some adjustment on your part if, for instance, the cost of hiring a stand suddenly goes up, this can be passed on to your customer. If you have quoted the final figure, any additional rise in stand hire cost would have to be absorbed by yourself. A quote or an estimate can be modified if your customer wants to change anything and you would then need to re-quote or adjust your estimate.

Whether you provide a quote or an estimate, make sure you state in your terms and conditions what your policy is regarding alterations. This is then clear to all parties when an order is accepted.

Requesting a deposit

It is always advisable to request a non-refundable deposit. This is your insurance that someone is serious about booking your time and skill. You will doubtless be spending time planning and possibly baking, well ahead of the delivery date and you do not want to find that all this effort goes unrewarded.

Taking a non-refundable deposit will also give you some income should an order fall through due to the customer withdrawing. You should state in your terms and conditions that a non-returnable deposit is payable and what percentage of the estimate or quote that might be.

A commonly requested deposit is around 20% to 25%, but you might be providing fruits cakes, cooked well in advance, or making detailed models months before the required date. You may wish to request a much higher deposit, maybe 50%, to cover your outlay in money and time, and to prevent you being left out of pocket if the event is cancelled.

You may personally choose to allow certain exceptions to the non-refundable deposit if you are flexible with your terms, for example, if cancellation was due to a bereavement. This is entirely at your own discretion.

State that full payment is due with no refund available from 28 days prior to the delivery date. Also state that, if you receive an order within 28 days of the delivery date, that in those circumstances, full non-refundable payment is expected with the order.

Cancellation policies

It is wise to put something in your terms and conditions explaining your policy on cancellation. State that your customer can cancel a contract at any time up to 28 days prior to the delivery date with the loss of the deposit, and that if the contract is cancelled after this time, then full payment is expected.

A customer does not have to give any reason for cancellation. However, a brief explanation will help you to improve the service you offer to customers in the future.

It may be that cancellation is due to unforeseen circumstances like flooding or illness, and you may be able to accommodate a new date or a change of venue. If not, you might consider being more flexible with the cancellation cost, depending upon the state of your order book!

Do not be too keen to retain full payment of an unfulfilled order if there is a reasonable chance that this may reflect badly upon your business. As far as possible, try to accommodate and assist your customer positively to leave a lasting good impression of you and your service.

Delivery policies

Make it clear to your customer what is included and what is not. Delivery can be easily overlooked. I price delivery separate from the cake cost so it can be taken as an optional extra. Some cakes may require an additional set-up cost and this should also be made clear on your customer's estimate or quote.

Delivery may include a time element as well as a cost or pence per mile. Remember that while you are driving a cake to a venue you are unable to bake another. This is all time, that you are spending for your business on your customer's order and is therefore part of the cost of that cake.

You may choose to offer a local delivery service free of charge, but again, be careful not to overlook set-up time even if the delivery is free. For cake decorators, this time is often at a weekend or towards the evening. Most people would not generally wish to work at these hours unpaid.

Customers may collect cakes, but be sure they understand fully, that the responsibility for the cake, once it is in their hands, rests entirely with them. You cannot be held responsible for a cake once it has left your premises. If your customer leaves the cake in the car on a hot day, while they go shopping, they can not blame you for it's subsequent demise.

I would always prefer to have the customer sign their acknowledgement of responsibility on a disclaimer form in the same way as when handing the responsibility over to catering or hotel staff at a venue. This disclaimer will also tell them of any inedible elements needing to be removed before serving the cake.

It is a good idea to check with any customer who is collecting a cake, that they know how to set the cake up or that they have someone happy to do this, who knows what they are doing. This is particularly relevant to wedding cakes with several tiers and possibly models and flowers to be added also.

A photograph of the final set-up can be a useful way of providing instruction, though sometimes the mention of what is required sends them running back to you with a request that you set the cake up. After all, most brides, their mums or anyone organising a party will generally not want any additional pressure or worry on their special day and may well appreciate your service to deliver and set up.

Tastings and viewings

Sometimes customers request a cake tasting. If you are asked for a tasting, do all you can to accommodate the customer. Denying them may create an unfavourable impression that you are hiding something, or that your product is in some way inferior.

It is important to ask before the tasting, if there are any particular requests, for example no nuts, flavour of jam with the filling, dietary needs etc. (be very careful about any guarantee of no nuts, an environment which uses nuts in cakes and marzipan will never be totally nut free).

If you can, try and fit the tasting in when you are already cooking a similar cake, this will save costs. Always offer the best pieces of cake to your customer, not the corner of a square cake! You do not need to offer iced cake unless they specifically request it.

Never post samples for tasting. You do not know how they will be treated whilst in transit. You may lose an order just because the postman fell on the box or the parcel sat in his van on a very hot day, spoiling your cake. This is your business reputation, do you really want to risk it? Customers will usually be understanding of your position.

Occasionally you may be asked if a viewing of the finished cake is possible. It is often the case that the cake will not be completed until it is set up on the day and therefore, the customer may not be able to view the completed cake. However I would still accept a viewing of the near-complete cake with the understanding that it may not be entirely finished.

If you refuse a viewing it may create an unwanted impression that you have something to hide! It may also lower your clients' perception of the quality of your product. If you are open and honest with your customers they will trust you and a good working relationship may well lead to future orders and recommendations.

Chapter 13

Designing Cakes for Customers

Tips when Designing a Cake

People often have a clear idea of the design they want. A bride may tell you the number of tiers they would like. It is very much a personal choice, but it is possible that you are being asked to produce a very large or tall cake with five or six layers of cake for an occasion with only a small number of guests. A fantastically large cake may be requested to give impact. In these instances, consider replacing some of the cake with polystyrene dummies.

Your customer may be totally unaware of the option to use dummies and your suggestion may give a new perspective on the cake design.

When designing cakes think about your own sugar crafting abilities. Consider how you might use skills that you are most confident with and enjoy doing. Be realistic and do not take on something involving skills you do not presently have. A simple design, well executed will result in a beautiful cake – and possibly save you the unnecessary stress of a more complicated or over ambitious design.

If you are proposing a skill that you are less confident with, then make sure you give yourself time to practice before having to commit to the cake. Think very carefully about what you are taking on considering your level of skill and your order book. Do you actually have the time to research and learn a new skill if it is required.

Sometimes it may be best to be totally honest. If your customer wants a wired spray of roses and you have never made a single rose, say so. You may feel confident to say that you will have that ability by the time the cake is required, or you may be able to offer an alternative design. But there may also be occasions when it is best to acknowledge that you may not be the best person to take on that particular order.

Working with dummies

Once iced and decorated, dummy cakes can look just like real ones and no-one need know. There will be less wasted cake but impact can be retained whilst enabling you to get some of the work done well in advance of the required delivery date. Dummies may also help you to build more stable structures for unusual shaped cakes.

Dummies can also be a very useful way of creating some images for your portfolio if you are starting from scratch. They also provide fantastic opportunities for practise and you can use them to create show pieces for exhibitions or even within your own premises.

Remember dummies can be stripped down and redecorated time and time again as the seasons change, you develop a new range or want to practise new ideas. Do not forget that they can be used in place of cake where a customer may require an impressive cake but may have a smaller number of guests to serve.

Dummies can also be used as separators between cakes and can be easily bought at various sizes and depths. There a masses of different shapes available from ducks to hearts! You may find an occasion when using a pre-shaped dummy allows you much more ease and time to develop a complex piece and even create pieces that your customers can keep as a memento of their event.

Elements of the design

As a business, you want your products to stand out, be original and unique. It is not recommended to copy cake designs originated by others. Try to produce an original design for every customer, although you may choose to have a 'standard' range of designs that can be adapted to most individual personal requirements.

On many occasions, a customer will come to you with set ideas or even a photograph of what they want. A bride may arrive with pictures of a cakes they like or even specify that they want 'that exact cake design'. If this is the case, I would suggest interpreting the design in such a way as to make it personal to them. I would also state that I do not 'copy' other peoples designs but will create an original design for them possibly using another design as inspiration, but adding elements and variations that are particular to them, for example, colour choice, initials, flowers etc..

On other occasions, a customer may have no ideas at all and may need your input to develop a suitable design. Your customer may have hobbies, jobs or interests that could form aspects of an original cake design. A party costume or a bride's dress design could inspire you. Bows, embroidery, lace or flowers, fabric colours and designs can all be used as reference. The initials of the recipient(s), or dates for a christening or wedding day are other possibilities for consideration to add personal touches.

Many customers will develop themes for their occasion. Some themes may be based on fairy tales, a winter wonderland or Gothic imagery for example. Other themes may be inspired by the location or venue, for example, a castle, beach, baronial hall or a converted barn – any of these could be used as inspiration to add personal touches or a bit of fun into your design. Some themes are based around a colour, or a theme like music, theatre, gardens, countries and even pets! Conversations with your customers will help you identify things which might inspire you to create a personal, appropriate and individual design.

Balance and proportion

Any cake should be well proportioned whatever the structure and this is largely down to the make-up of the design. You do not want to find your eyes being constantly drawn to any particular point, unless, of course, that is what was intended. You need to create a well planned and balanced design.

If you are planning a complicated structure or a lot of added decorations or models, consider the overall physical balance and structural stability of the final piece as well as the final appearance.

Detailed side designs may be lost under a mass of trailing flowers, but a very simple side design could set off an elegant tall spray of flowers on the top of a beautifully iced cake. For practical reasons you will also want to consider the type of side design you are using, for example, fine piped extension work combined with trailing flowers may be a disaster waiting to happen. Make sure any tall construction is well supported and balanced. Try not to create problems for yourself and bear in mind the transportation and delivery of your cake creation while you are designing it.

Stability of very tall cakes is an important consideration, especially if they are sponge. Dowelling will provide vital support but multi-tiered cakes need to be very stable and careful consideration should be given to the display position. A cake stand, incorporated as part of your design, could add extra stability for taller cakes and may also dispense with the need for dowelling.

Cake stands and knives

Traditionally, large silver cake stands have often been used to display wedding cakes. These are sometimes used for anniversary and other occasion cakes. Check if your customer actually wants to use one of these heavy silver base stands. They often do not fit in with the theme of the occasion or cake style but many venues may assume it is required. If your customer does wish to use one, check the exact size of cake board that will fit on the stand as many will not take cake boards over 16".

There are many different ways to display cakes or simply raise them for greater impact. Do not be restricted by tradition or just because there is a traditional base stand available. Quite elaborate stands can quite easily be made using polystyrene dummies with fabric and all sorts of other items.

Cake boards, separators, stands, vases, flowers (artificial, real or sugar), numerous craft items, paints, beads, even plaster of Paris can be used to present your cake if you are of a creative mind! As long as your cake is sitting on a food safe surface, you can put this onto any display you like. This may add to the individual nature and look of cakes supplied by your business.

Your cake design may require a specific cake stand to display the cake, consider whether you need to hire this. If you do need to hire one, book it early as stands get booked months in advance. If you have your own to offer, make sure you note which cake stand is booked for which date to avoid double booking. Buy any materials needed well in advance of the date to leave nothing to chance.

Check if a cake knife is needed. Many venues will offer their own but it is worth checking. If the venue does not have a cake knife, your customer may need to hire one unless she can hire from you. Once again, make sure bookings are made early to avoid disappointment.

Make sure you make it clear who is responsible for returning the stand and/or knife after the occasion. Confirm by what time it should be returned to you or the company who supplied it.

Flowers

If you are dealing with a florist regarding fresh flowers for the cake, it is advisable to give the florist a copy of the design details stating exactly what the flower requirements are.

Fresh flowers can add the perfect touch to a beautiful wedding cake. The flowers can be taken care of by the cake maker or the florist, or even a bride's family for example. Make sure these decisions are made clear to everyone involved.

Some flowers are entirely edible. These can often be found in grocery stores. If you choose edible flowers to place on a cake they should be ready to use as soon as you take them out of the container. Be sure to use flowers that you are absolutely positive are edible varieties and have grown free of pesticides.

Common edibles flowers include day lilies, dianthus, lilacs, pansies and roses. Other varieties of flowers are toxic, but still frequently used for cakes. These include calla lilies, hyacinths, lily of the valley, tulips, hydrangeas, bird of paradise and carnations. Ivy can also be toxic.

Any variety of flower, whether known to be toxic or not, may be safe in theory, but may have been tainted with pesticides used while they were growing. For this reason, it is important to ask your floral supplier about the origins of any flower that might come in contact with your cake surface.

There are poisonous flowers and foliage which should be avoided but if you do not have the knowledge yourself, your florist should be able to advise you on this if necessary. Do your research and ask plenty of questions before placing any type of flower against your cake. Remember, your florist is the flower expert, although the purchase of a good quality floristry book can prove very useful to any serious cake decorator.

For years, numerous toxic flowers have been used on cakes, removed, and the cakes eaten with no incident but many would say fresh flowers are more trouble than they are worth.

Check carefully, and get your customer's full understanding about the flowers required. Does your customer really want fresh flowers on their cake if some may be toxic or even poisonous? If their answer is no, then sugar or artificial flowers may be a suitable alternatives. However, you will still find a large number of customers still wishing to follow the old traditions to use fresh flowers on cakes.

Use your disclaimer to give details about fresh flowers used on cakes, particularly if any are inserted into flower picks inserted in the cake.

Flower solutions and alternatives

If fresh flowers are required, use a small, inconspicuous barrier to keep the flowers from directly touching the cake. An inexpensive, easy-to-find, option would be to use something like a jam jar lid or trimmed base of a plastic carton. When positioned well, the lid or base will disappear under the flowers. A disc of waxed paper may be sufficient under a small posy. A jam jar lid or cut off base of a plastic cup or container, can also be wrapped in ribbon if necessary.

If you would rather not risk fresh flowers or it seems like a lot of trouble to determine which flowers might be safe for the cake, you could choose silk flowers. These days many higher quality silk flowers have a remarkably life-like appearance, so if you choose well, no one will notice that the flowers are not real.

Keep in mind, however, that it may be difficult to determine whether artificial flowers have been exposed to anything toxic during the manufacturing process. For this reason, it is still wise to use an inconspicuous barrier between the silk flowers and the cake as you would for fresh flowers.

Sugar flowers which are wired individually or into sprays are clearly not edible. Some sugar flowers are made using polystyrene cones, kebab sticks or cocktail sticks in their construction, but many can be made without using any inedible items. These unwired sugar flowers can sit directly upon cakes and are totally edible.

A significant advantage of sugar flowers, whether wired or not, is that you can make them at a scale to suit the size of the cake. Some real blooms are far too large for most cakes, but by using sugar flowers, you can create them at a size that suits your customer's cake design.

If you intend to insert flowers, whether fresh, artificial or wired sugar, into a cake, you must use a flower pick. This is a plastic tube, closed and usually pointed at the base. It is inserted into the cake to hold flower stems whilst protecting the cake from wires, stems and other inedible matter. The pick will also prevent air (and potentially, bacteria) from gaining access to the cake under the icing.

Flower picks come in a large variety of sizes so that tiny, or quite large sprays of flowers can be securely attached. Sometimes a flower pick is too long for the depth of a cake. If you need to reduce the length, make sure you cut off from the top, open end of the pick, to retain the closed tip that will protect the cake.

Positioning flowers

Flower picks can be used to fix flowers in a large variety of positions on cakes. They may be used to secure larger sprays of flowers on the 'shoulders' of a stacked wedding cake or in a central spray on the top of a cake. Tall cakes may have a cascading waterfall of flowers secured in several flower picks on the cake's sides. Small lid type containers can be used where the flowers can simply sit on the surface of cakes.

Neatly taped wired flowers can be secured using royal icing upon the surface of a cake as long as the wires do not penetrate the surface of the cake's icing. Remember not to stick wired flowers directly into cakes. If you need to create many standing stems, you may need to attach them to a separate cake card to hold the flowers and this can then be positioned on top of the cake keeping wires away from the cake.

Other items requiring wired supports should also be inserted into flower picks. For example, a figurine may need additional support inserted in the cake. A kebab or cocktail stick does not require you to use a flower pick for protection but wires must be kept away from the cake. I would still be very careful to tell my customer of any inedible items used on their cake whether flower picks are used or not.

You may have room to place flowers between the layers. Blooms can be used to fill the space between tiers of cake. Fresh flower heads, cut with just a short stem, will last surprisingly well simply pushed into the space between tiers. They can be positioned onto a sheet of waxed paper to prevent anything being transferred onto the cake's surface. Take care that the paper will not be visible and is well hidden behind the flower heads.

It is a good idea when booking the delivery time with the venue, to plan the set-up of a cake with the florist in mind, especially if you are receiving flowers from them for the cake. You might be able to meet at the venue, but you will need to make sure you do not arrive before them if you need flowers to complete the cake. You may have time to bring the flowers together on the cake while the florist is still on hand to help if there are any issues.

Bear in mind that you do not want to be setting up a cake whilst a florist is trailing flowers over beams above or attaching flowers around the cake table! There may be some instances where it is wise to make sure that venue flowers are complete, mist-sprayed, and are no longer dripping before you set up a cake anywhere near them!

Discuss the options with your florist well in advance to ensure all goes right on the day of setting up.

Chapter 14

And Finally . . .

You are your Business.

There are no short cuts and you will need to put all your effort into building and maintaining your business.

It will involve a great many hours of research preparation and planning. But remember, the rewards can be just as great.

All that is needed now is to wish you every success for a fulfilling and successful business adventure.

Chapter 15

Helpful Contacts

Where you can get Further Advice

There is a vast range of advice and guidelines available on the Food Standards Agency's website: www.food.gov.uk or via your local authority environmental health department.

If you run a small catering business, there are packs available to help you put in place food safety management procedures based on the principles of HACCP as previously mentioned. These packs have been produced by the FSA and you can find details of them at www.food.gov.uk/business-industry/caterers/haccp/

Food industry guides

There are a number of FSA publications that you might find helpful. These include:
- 'Starting up – Your first steps to running a catering business' This invaluable publication for those starting a new food business is available via www.food.gov.uk/starting-up
- 'Food law inspections and your business' is available via www.food.gov.uk/food-law-inspections

Guides produced by the food industry also give advice on how to comply with food hygiene regulations. Using the guides is voluntary, but they are officially recognised by the Government, and enforcement officers are required to take them into account when assessing whether businesses comply with the regulations. For full details visit food.gov.uk/industryguides

Useful contacts

Chartered Trading Standards Institute:
www.tradingstandards.uk

HM Customs and Revenue:
www.hmrc.gov.uk

Food Standards Agency (FSA):
www.fsa.gov.uk

National Business Register:
www.start.biz/National_Business_Reg

Companies House:
www.companieshouse.gov.uk

Health and Safety Authority (HSA):
www.hsa.i.e./eng

County Council Trading Standards:
via your local county council

Borough Council Environmental Health Authority:
via your local borough council

The Federation of Small Businesses:
membership@fsb.org.uk Tel: 01253 336000

Food Standards Agency:
infocentre@foodstandards.gsi.gov.uk Tel: 0207 276 8181

Health and Safety Executive:
hse.infoline@natbrit.com Tel: 0845 345 0055

The British Sugarcraft Guild:
www.bsg.co.uk

All the information is available to anyone and mostly free.

Awarding Bodies that provide information about training for food handlers:

HABC - Highfield Awarding Body for Compliance:
www.highfieldabc.com
UK's leading supplier of compliance qualifications

CIEH - The Chartered Institute of Environmental Health:
www.cieh.org
An independent organization representing the interests of the environmental health profession.

REHIS - The Royal Environmental Health Institute of Scotland:
www.rehis.com
An independent, Scottish charity whose main objectives are for the advancement of Environmental Health.

RSPH - The Royal Society for Public Health:
www.rsph.org.uk
An independent charity dedicated to the promotion and protection of public health and wellbeing.

BII - British Institute of Innkeepers:
www.bii.org
Professional trade association which includes professional qualifications.

HSE - Health & Safety Executive:
www.hse.gov.uk
The national independent watchdog for work-related health, safety and illness.

Public Service Ombudsmen:

England Local Government Ombudsman: www.lgo.org.uk

Scotland Public Services Ombudsman: www.spso.org.uk

Wales Public Services Ombudsman: www.ombudsman-wales.org.uk

Northern Ireland Ombudsman: www.ni-ombudsman.org.uk

Glossary/Bibliography

Information in this guide is extracted from:

The Chartered Trading Standards Institute:
www.tradingstandards.uk

HM Customs and Revenue:
www.hmrc.gov.uk

Food Standards Agency (FSA):
www.fsa.gov.uk

National Business Register:
www.start.biz/National_Business_Reg

Companies House:
www.companieshouse.gov.uk

Health and Safety Authority (HSA):
www.hsa.i.e./eng

Surrey County Council Trading Standards:
www.surreycc.gov.uk/business-and-consumers/trading-standards

Guildford Borough Council Environmental Health Authority:
www.guildford.gov.uk/environmentalhealth

The British Sugarcraft Guild:
www.bsg.co.uk

Index

Lightning Source UK Ltd.
Milton Keynes UK
UKOW07f0552091215

264406UK00014B/201/P